Mermaid
Magic

Also by Amy Sophia Marashinsky

The Goddess Oracle

Amy Sophia Marashinsky

Mermaid Magic

all about mermaids
and how to bring
their magic into
your life

HARPER
element

HarperElement
An Imprint of HarperCollins*Publishers*
77–85 Fulham Palace Road
Hammersmith, London W6 8JB

The website address is:
www.thorsonselement.com

and *HarperElement* are trademarks of
HarperCollins*Publishers* Limited

First published by HarperElement 2005

13 5 7 9 10 8 6 4 2

Illustrations by Audrey Botha at Wheelhouse Creative Ltd.
Illustrations taken from *A Mermaid's Journey* by Beatrice Kidd

A catalogue record of this book
is available from the British Library

ISBN 0 00 721082 5

Printed and bound in Great Britain by
Martins The Printers, Berwick Upon Tweed

For my parents, Myra and Julius Marashinsky,
with gratitude and love for all they did.

Contents

Acknowledgements viii
Introduction xiii

Chapter One   All About Mermaids 1
Chapter Two   Daily Contact with Mermaids 15
Chapter Three Mermaid Magic for Love and Sex 59
Chapter Four   Mermaid Magic for Protection
                   and Personal Power 127
Chapter Five   Mermaid Magic for Prosperity
                   and Life Purpose 175
Appendix   Mermaids and Lunar Magic 218

Notes 238
Resource Guide 240
Bibliography 243
Author Biography 248

Acknowledgements

First and foremost I want to thank my commissioning editor Katy Carrington for asking me to write *Mermaid Magic*. She is the one you must appreciate most for the fact that *Mermaid Magic* exists. Then comes my editor Susanna Abbott, who helped me through the process, read the manuscript over and over and over again, answered questions, sparked creativity. If you find this book well done, you can send your accolades to her. Lastly, though not leastly, of my crew at HarperElement, I want to sing symphonies of high praise and earth-shaking appreciation for Jo Kyle, who was my copy editor. If the book has a consistent, fun and whimsical tone, then murmur your thanks in her direction.

I want to thank someone who has not been thanked enough, and that is Larry Machiz. I was working for Larry as his legal secretary in 1995–6 while writing *The Goddess*

Oracle. Larry supported me financially both with legal work and with an absence of legal work and plenty of spare time to write *TGO*. Without being supported by Larry there would be no *The Goddess Oracle* and Harper-Collins UK would not have acquired it, Katy would not have become acquainted with my work and I would not have been asked to write this little book.

There are my writer/artist friends who spent time with me on the phone, allayed my doubts, fed me encouraging words and were very supportive. They are Gary Meitrott, Hrana Janto, Dave Sheppard, Kip Rosser, Ted Enik and John Bailey.

Next come the members of Sirius Community, an intentional spiritual community, where I live. I felt the loving support of the entire community of twenty strong behind me. Those that stand out are: Ernesto Santamaria, who came and lovingly cleaned my house and gave me marketing advice; Brian Hydefrost, who took care of me (and my cats) daily by bringing me wood, cleaning the cat box, doing other odd jobs so I could keep my fingers to the grindstone; Katylist Kombucha, who provided me with ginger kombucha that rallied and recharged my flagging energy; Will Savage, who was backup for Brian and who loaned me samples of real amber; author Jill Kelly, who always knew what I was going through; core group members, Bruce Davidson, Linda Reimer, Deborah and Brice Wilson, who approved my leave of absence so I could write this book, and massage therapist and energy worker extraordinaire, Erin Blocker. Being a spiritual community, my community mates also held energy for me on the inner planes. For this I sing your praises.

Next on my list is Christopher Allan, my photographer, friend and Lyme support person. For some strange reason, knowing that what I was experiencing was 'typical' to Lyme always made me feel better.

Thanks also go to Barrett Briggs and Blaire Robey, who built my infrared electric light sauna. I sauna-ed twice daily and could not have written *Mermaid Magic* without it.

To Josephine Davidson, writer and Sirius Community member, and recovering-writer Tom Cumella, who listened, listened, listened, read and commented on my manuscript, and dispensed much needed advice, deep,

deep thanks from never-ending wells of gratitude for giving so much of your time and energy to me and my process.

For my beloved cats, Shiva and Lakota, catnip bushels of appreciation for the patience you showed me when I wrote past your dinner time, for the forbearance you extended to me when you allowed me to sleep late and through your breakfast time, and for merging your creative energy with mine, in the clever guise of sleeping on my wrists as I typed.

To all the mermaids and mermaid goddesses, I am grateful to you for being willing to make magic through me.

Please know that you were all needed and are all deeply appreciated. I could not have done what I did if you didn't do what you did.

Introduction

Welcome to the delightful and delicious, fun and frolicking world of making magic with mermaids. Mermaids have floated in and out of our consciousness for centuries, inspiring us with their beauty and luring us because they embody what we have lost, **the 'wild feminine': the part of a woman that is free, natural and deeply alive.**

In this book you will be guided step by step through everything you need to know to enable you to work magic simply, easily and safely with these marvellous beings from the sea. As you swim through these pages you will uncover the sunken, hidden treasure of what mermaids really are, their history, and most significant, how developing a relationship with mermaids can transform your life!

As you dive deep into this book you will learn how to connect with your Inner Mermaid, your own source of the 'wild feminine'; meet some mermaid goddesses who can be invoked to assist you in love and sexuality, prosperity, inspiration and creativity, and other areas of your life; discover lunar mermaid magic, which engages the energy of the moon's cycles to power-up your rituals for dynamic results, and be inspired with fun, creative projects, like creating a mermaid altar, making a mermaid necklace and recipes for food and baths that weave the presence and magic of mermaids into the daily fabric of your life.

Before we get started, I would like to define a few terms that I use in *Mermaid Magic* so that we can be on the same page. Mermaid is defined in the Oxford Dictionary as 'a mythical sea creature with a woman's head and trunk and a fish's tail'. My explanation of mermaid is that part of women that is uninhibited, self-willed, virgin (meaning whole and complete unto herself), primary, essential, unmixed, raw and real. **Mermaids are *par excellence* the archetypical image**

and symbol of the feminine and all that it embodies: sensuality, nurturing, mothering, power, sexuality, mystery, spirituality and magic.

This brings us to magic. Magic is the transformation of energy from one state to another. Magic is making manifest what you want to bring into form. Magic is also the conscious use of your will, your focus or your intent to positively affect an outcome. So when I use the term 'magic' I mean working with your intent. Your intent is what you want or what is needed by you.

Mermaids are magical beings. And one way to get more magic in your life is to gain the assistance of magical beings.

Creating mermaid magic

The first step in creating mermaid magic is getting clarity on what you need. After you know what you need and have expressed that need clearly – and here I suggest that you keep a journal and write that need down – then you can form your intent. For example, let's say you need more money. That means you intend to be prosperous. OK, now you can do a ritual for financial abundance and prosperity. But don't stop there!!! You need to expect that good will come. Expect that you will be given what you need. You may not know exactly what needs to happen or what you need to do to increase your finances. You don't need to know the 'how'. That is up to the Divine, up to the Goddess. All you need to do is know you have a need and be clear about that need.

Your intention then is to have more money. Now that you intend to have more money, everything in your life needs to resonate to the key of prosperity. Looking again at your need for more money, do you spend the day thinking about how little you have or do your thoughts serenade the Divine with thanks for the abundance in your life?

Magic involves two particular attitudes. The first attitude is expectancy. After you do your magic, you then expect that things are going to come in a fabulous way. All you need to do is let go of how they should come. Just know they will come and expect the best. The second is after your magic has come to fruition, then you need to spend time in an attitude of gratitude. Living with thanks for everything that comes your way will open the floodgates and ensure that more will come your way.

Magic and ritual need to be fun. If it's a chore or a dirge or becomes one more thing you have to do, don't do it. With that attitude toward magic, that is what you will create! Cultivate a sense of fun, a sense of delight. Magic invokes the creative part of you to come out and play.

Since one of the areas that mermaids rule is the realm of the senses, it is vitally important when making mermaid magic to engage all of your senses. So give yourself permission to be sensuous. This is because the more you involve your senses, the stronger and more effective your magic will be. *Mermaid Magic* was written to appeal and engage all of your senses: smell, touch, taste, sight and sound as well as your three bodies: your physical body, your emotional body and your mental body.

Rituals, journeys and invocations

Throughout this book you will find rituals, journeys (guided meditations) and invocations to help you contact mermaids and gain their assistance to bring magic into your daily life.

Ritual is the doing of certain acts that will focus your energy and help bring about your intent. Ritual is the play that you do to help the magic happen. And here you may be asking the question: do we need to have ritual items, clothing, objects etc.? No; however, if they help bring out our creative and playful, uninhibited sides, then, YES we need them! It is up to you. There are those who can make magic with the barest of altars and there are others for whom the use of wands, magical clothing (which is clothing that is consecrated for use only during rituals and often made by the person herself), gems, jewellery, statues, flowers, stones, different water from sacred wells, make up, etc., and whatever else can be imagined, is a must. Experiment and see what works for you. That is the most important thing. There are lots of fun ideas for ritual items, mermaid altars and so on throughout the book.

A **journey** is a guided meditation in which you go somewhere. Its purpose is to release you from your conscious life and take you into the unconscious where you can effect transformation in your life. Since the unconscious is often thought of as water, mermaids are the perfect beings to assist you in getting to the deep levels of yourself.

All the journeys in *Mermaid Magic* are written using the same language and words to take you into an altered state and bring you back from the altered state. This is to facilitate your journeying and make it easy for you to develop the skill of accessing your unconscious in this way. There is a rhythm, too, in the word choice and its occasional repetition that swoops you up and takes you away. It is not meant to appeal to the linear left-brain but rather be evocative and easily read by the mystical right-brain.

It might be helpful to record all the journeys in this book on a cassette tape, so that you when you are ready to swim with the mermaids during your journey time, you can do so without being tied to the dry land of a book. You may also want to invest in a cassette tape or CD of ocean sounds to use during your journeys and at other times.

During a journey, the mermaid you are journeying to meet may ask you for something (a 'gift'). Know that the response you need to give will effortlessly and easily come from you during the journey. Also know that whatever shape or form the response takes is exactly what is needed.

An **invocation** is a poem or words put together to ask sincerely, politely and lovingly for a particular energy to come and be with you. You need not use my invocations. I have put them there as a starting or jumping off point for you. When you have become acquainted with the mermaid goddesses, by all means use your own words, or continue to use mine, as you wish.

The rituals and journeys in this book require privacy and time when you will not be disturbed by anything or anyone. Of course you may do the rituals and journeys with a friend or a group of your mermaid friends, but by privacy I mean a quiet and conducive space.

Keeping a journal

All you need to get started to make mermaid magic is simple: you just need yourself and you need to make the time. You will also need to commit to a diary or journal. Keeping a journal is a great way to track your transformation. You will want to make notes of what happened after a particular ritual or journey. Reading and putting into practice the ideas in *Mermaid Magic* will stir your inner cauldron and bring lots of creative ideas bubbling to the surface and you will want to record them. The mermaids will be speaking with you and you need to write down what they are saying.

Are you ready for mermaid magic?

The questions you need to ask yourself are: 'Am I ready to accept responsibility for myself and enlist the aid of the mermaids? Am I ready to rediscover and live life from my wild feminine? Am I ready to integrate my wild feminine?

Am I ready to accept assistance from the mermaids? Am I ready to contact mermaids? I am ready to do what it takes to transform my life? Am I willing to transform? Am I willing to partner with mermaids to transform?' Mermaids can help but they can't do the job alone. It is a partnership we are creating here. The question you need to ask and answer is, are you willing and open?

About this book

As you will see, this book is divided up into chapters, three of which deal with particular areas of your life – love and sexuality; protection and personal power, and prosperity and life purpose. There is also a chapter devoted to the herstory of mermaids and another on how to contact mermaids and bring them into your daily life. Included in this chapter is a section on lunar magic, with the specifics of working lunar magic in an Appendix.

The chapters are packed with journeys, rituals, activities, tips, **Mermaid Interludes**, which are legends, stories or tales about mermaids, and **Mythological Moments**, which come before each journey and contain mythology and bits of pertinent information about the mermaid goddess that you will meet in your meditation.

You can buy the ingredients listed throughout this book on-line or at your local arts and crafts and health food stores. We all know that mermaids live in the oceans. What we might not know is whatever we purchase, from food, to laundry detergents, to gardening supplies, make-up, etc., degrades and ends up in the ocean in one form or another. Let's keep our oceans safe for our mermaid sisters by choosing organic, if available.

In the 'Resources Guide' section at the end of the book, you will find websites you can visit to find the ingredients mentioned here. If they are not listed for where you live, then you can do a search on the internet for them. If you are low on funds don't worry about having to purchase anything. You can do wonderfully effective magic with mermaids without a spending a single sou.

There are as many mermaid goddesses as there are different cultures that have a seacoast. The ones that are included in this book are therefore a small sampling. Making magic with mermaids/mermaid goddesses involves creating a relationship with them. They are quite willing to come to your assistance when called upon, but it is up to you to make the first move and open the door.

An harm ye none

All magic is done with the knowledge: **an harm ye none**. Because when you do magic, there is one finger pointing out and three fingers pointing back at you. Which means anything you put out comes back to you threefold. In *Mermaid Magic* all magic is white magic or done for personal transformation. It is also to be done with the intent of the 'highest good for all'. All the rituals and journeys in *Mermaid Magic* are done with you surrounded in white light and this offers protection from any free-floating astral energies and earmarks your magic for positive benefits.

So, all this being said, if you are ready to meet the mermaids and have a magical, delectable time, read on!

CHAPTER 1

All About Mermaids

The heartbeat of the mother, thump-thump, thump-thump, like the echo of waves pounding on a distant shore, is the first sound that humans hear, while enveloped in their ocean of amniotic water. Thump-thump, thump-thump. It creates a deep yearning for the sea and anything to do with water.

For women, the pull of the ocean's tides in a distinct rhythm with the moon's cycles, are mirrored in our bodies by our own cycles.

There is a story told by ancient women wise and strong with farseeing eyes, that each daughter born on land carries a secret thread that binds her to the sea. Binds her to a watery, elemental version of herself, of her own wild feminine nature, hidden and slumbering, that lives in the deeps, the ocean, the unconscious, the water. It is the charge of that land-born daughter to seek out the blue-green strand and reclaim that wild piece of herself, the mermaid, that dwells in the sea. It is also said that for those who make the journey, the rewards are abundantly magical . . .

Herstory

Older than time itself, mermaids have been with us forever. The names of the ancient goddess known as Marratu to the Chaldeans, Marah to the Jews, Mariham to the Persians, Mary to the Christians, all derived from Mari, meaning sea or waters. As you can see, even the oldest goddesses had names that referred to the sea. According to Barbara G. Walker in *The Women's Encyclopedia of Myths and Secrets*, 'She was also the Great Fish who gave birth to the gods, later [known as] the Mermaid . . .'[1] The original symbol for the astrological sign of Pisces in Lemurian[2] times was a mermaid. Many of the half-man, half-fish gods, like Oannes, for example, the Sumerian god, hail back to an older divinity, that being the Goddess.

In the beginning, our ancestors worshipped the goddess. She was known in many shapes, many forms, to many different cultures by many different names. She was the personification of the Feminine Divine. It was She who created the world. It was She who gave birth to the gods. It was She as Great Mother, Earth, Ocean, Sun, Moon, Universe, Everything, for everything was Her. In time She gave birth to a consort, or son. And it was he from around 4000–2000 BCE whose culture took over and replaced the civilization of the Goddess.

As is true for any take-over, whether it be political or corporate or marital – as in the case of a divorce, or the exchange of property or sale of a house – there is change. What was before is no longer and what is new rules. When the religions that focused on a god took over from the cultures that were matrilineal, the Goddess was demoted and women lost their power. History is always written by the victors.

Prior to this gradual change in focus from matrilineal to patrilineal, women could do anything and be anything. They owned land, were judges, priestesses, artisans, politicians, ran companies, cared for their children, ruled countries. As did men. In the civilizations of the Goddess artistic expression was essential, and relations between the genders were sexy and playful.

Afterwards, as the Goddess was relegated to wife, and little else, so were women. Emphasis on artistic expression was replaced with focus on war and weapons. Sex was deliberately corrupted out of fear of the power of the feminine: from ecstatic union, gift of the Goddess, to shameful, sinful and base. This was a slow but drastic change. In ancient times the Goddess represented fertility, sexuality, sensuality, power, wisdom, sovereignty, abundance, creativity.

'In Northern Babylonia, Eve was known as "the Divine Lady of Eden", or "Goddess of the Tree of Life".'[3] Later, in the Old Testament of the Bible, Goddess Eve was reduced to a rib and made responsible for humanity's expulsion from the garden of Eden, and for death. The Bible and early Christian theologians went on to characterize women as evil. 'Origen declared, "Matrimony is impure and unholy, a means of sexual passion."'[4] 'St. Augustine pronounced the doctrine that "concupiscence" is the root of original sin. . .'[5] Women and children had no rights and were given to man to be treated as his property.

Although the civilization of the Goddess was destroyed, She wasn't. She found expression in the cult of the Virgin Mary (again, Mari for the Sea Goddess) and all of her feared aspects were given to mermaids, who also became known as sirens – as in seducers of men – of the sea. The Goddess, the feminine, didn't disappear completely. Those wondrous qualities of the feminine, the Goddess – power, spirituality, sexuality, sensuousness, creativity, fertility and wisdom – found rich soil in the archetype[6] of the mermaid. There she survives, in our modern times, where she is still very much in our consciousness.

Mermaids in popular culture

The Little Mermaid by Hans Christian Andersen is one of the best loved stories. It clearly reflects the attitude of its time about mermaids, which was that they didn't possess a soul and only through marriage to a mortal man could they gain one. Not only was it a high-grossing Disney-produced animation, but the Little Mermaid character made a brief cameo appearance in that wildly popular mega bestseller, *The Da Vinci Code* by Dan Brown.

Prior to *The Little Mermaid*, there was the movie *Splash* in 1984, and *Million Dollar Mermaid* with swimming star Esther Williams in 1952. In the sixties there was Doris Day in the film *The Glass Bottom Boat*, and in the forties *Mr. Peabody and the Mermaid*. Another hugely successful book or books, I should say, is *The Harry Potter* series. In Book Four there are mer-folk living in the lake at Hogwarts and they are part of one of Harry's challenges.

Mermaid legends around the world

Mermaids appear in the legends and tales of cultures around the world. What is interesting to note is that the stories about them are consistent from country to country. All agree that if they marry a mortal man they will acquire a soul. The comb is a valued possession as is their mirror, said to be emblems of their vanity. These two items were related to the Goddess of Love, Aphrodite's toilet, and became part and parcel of mermaid paraphernalia. Irish mer-folk require a red cap in order to breathe under water, and if taken, will do anything to get it back.

They are loreley, nixies and *Meerjungfrauen* when in Germany. The Irish call them merrow. To the Scottish they are *Ceasg*, maid of the wave. In France and Haiti she is called *La Sirene*. Nereids are mermaids to the Greek. The Scandinavian have wave maidens and they are the daughters of the mermaid sea goddess Ran.

The Greeks spread tales that the waters surrounding their mainland and islands were overrun with fearsome and deadly monsters as a means of protection. Those aquatic singing sensations, the Sirens, first appeared in *The Odyssey* of Homer. They were half bird, half woman, fantastical beings with mesmerizing voices. Their singing lured men to their death.

The image of the siren gradually changed over the years and merged with the Goddess images of half woman, half fish. At first mermaids were said to be benign and helpful. When they became fused with the mythology of sirens, they became more dangerous.

Mermaids are weather workers and sighting them at sea portends foul weather. If you do them a good turn, they will reward you with either fabulous riches or grant one of your wishes. People whose living was made from the sea, like sailors and fishermen, would often appeal to mermaids for protection from harm and to ensure safe voyages.

Lonely, single men uninterested in mortal women of their acquaintance, were known to gamble their conjugal joy upon rare, alien women of exquisite beauty (mermaids) singing alone on a rock or dancing in a small circle of sisters on shore. The men knew that to catch mermaids required stealing their red cap, or comb or skin (fish or seal). Once caught, she would have to be his wife, until she found what was stolen from her. And when she did she went back to the sea for good.

There has never been a time in history when mermaids were thought not to exist. The earliest record of disbelief in mermaids began relatively recently, in the seventeenth century. Before then they were incorporated in *Natural History* written by Pliny the Elder in the first century A.D. They were sighted by two well-known explorers: Christopher Columbus on his voyage to America, during the late 1400s, recorded it in his sea-log and Henry Hudson and his crew received an eyeful in June, 1608. 'A law on the books in England until the twentieth century claimed for the crown "all mermaids found in British waters".'[7] And families who had members with a webbing of their hands and feet were thought to have a mermaid or two as an ancestor.

Mermaid Interlude: Melusine

The tale of Melusine or Melusina comes to us from four-teenth century France. In it Raymond, a French noble, goes out boar hunting with his friend, Emmerick. As we all know, boars can be especially dangerous to capture, because of their long, extremely sharp tusks and quick movements. After sighting the trail of the boar, Emmerick disappears into the forest after him. Upon hearing his friend's cries for help Raymond runs after him. He finds Emmerick and the boar struggling, and in the act of killing the boar, Raymond also accidentally kills his friend.

Mad with grief, Raymond wanders about the forest for days, not knowing how he can face Emmerick's family and tell them what occurred. One day he happens upon a woman of extraordinary beauty standing beside a sacred spring. She tells him her name, Melusine, offers him water and asks him his troubles. He confides in her and she comforts him. Impressed by her wisdom and beauty, he falls in love with her and asks her to marry him. She agrees upon one condition, that she have Saturdays off, and that he never ask her or seek to know what she does with her time.

Melusine uses her magical powers to build her and Raymond a glittering palace to live in, with her chambers encompassing the sacred spring. Raymond and Melusine are very happy together. They have children, some of whom are quite strange. One day after being goaded by his father about what Melusine does on her Saturdays, Raymond decides to find out. He spies on Melusine in her chambers having her Saturday bath and discovers she is half fish, dragon or serpent. He says nothing until one of their children burns down a monastery, then in wrath, he turns on her saying, 'this is your doing, you evil serpent.' As soon as the words are out of his mouth he regrets them, but it is too late. Melusine now knows that he has broken his promise to her. She assumes her real form and vanishes.

Melusine, in her own words

There is always one condition
when you wed the wild magical feminine
whether we have secret skins of feathers
fur
or scales
Always one condition
relating to our sovereignty
the right to do with our time
and ourselves
as we please
All I asked
was for one day
one day out of seven
one day for myself
one day to shake out
and not hide
my real nature
Not hide that part of myself
you would fear

one day to be wild
then I could be what you wanted
Didn't you wonder at who I really was
when I built for you that magnificent magical mansion
or were you so dazzled by form
that you didn't care then
to discover what lay beneath its veil
Was the price of one day too much to ask
for all that I abundantly gave and did
on the other six
that you could rend the happiness that was ours?
Or was the reality of my having that one measly day
this short piece of freedom
not devoted to you
beyond your knowing
out of your control
what you could not bear?

Now that we are acquainted with mermaids from a 'her-storical' perspective, we are ready get into the water and make contact.

CHAPTER 2

Daily Contact with Mermaids

Harnessing the power and magic of the mermaids can pull any life that is teetering on the brink of ho-hum-ness into full-fledged razzle-dazzle. Since mermaids are magical beings, the more you invite contact with them in your daily life, the more charged with magic your life will become.

In Chapter 1 we were introduced to the world of mermaids – we got our fins wet. Now in this chapter we will acquire the skills that we will be using in the rest of the book for contacting these magical beings. It is time for us to explore, to splash about, make some fun tools, learn some simple, easy and effective techniques, and let our imaginations and creativity bloom.

Mermaid Altars

Those lucky mermaid sisters who live on or near a beach seem to have it made. They have access to the ocean or lake and can spend time there soaking up those resonances with which to imbue their lives and their mermaid magic. That doesn't mean that the land-locked need to feel slighted. We can bring the essence of the sea into our homes and we do this with the creation of our altar.

Building a mermaid altar in your home is a terrific way to woo contact with those sea beings. It also presents a focal point for magical activity. Altars come in all shapes and sizes and can go wherever you need them to be. They can be on a table, on the floor, mounted on a wall, in a window treatment and in any room in your home, including the bathroom. They can even be in your closet, but use the closet only if you haven't outed yourself as a mermaid, yet.

The idea when creating your altar is to let your creativity out of its cage. Look at the space you inhabit and decide what would work best. If you live with others and share every inch of living quarters, it would be wise to have a discussion first, so you can reach a win-win situation for all as to the best place for your altar.

Once you have decided on the best place for your altar you are ready to get to work. Here are some suggestions for things you might want on your altar, to turbo-charge and inspire.

SUGGESTIONS FOR YOUR ALTAR

✦ *seashells*
✦ *sand from a beach, or create your own 'sand' (for example, you could use glitter – either one solid colour or a mix of different colours)*
✦ *candles (whatever colours appeal to you)*
✦ *your Inner Mermaid incense burner (see page 19)*
✦ *your mermaid power necklace (see page 142)*
✦ *driftwood*
✦ *stones – either collected at a beach or ones that speak to you that you pick up when you are either on a walk, in the garden or rambling about. Use what appeals to you and check in with the stone – by closing your eyes,*

taking a few deep breaths, asking the stone and listening for an answer – to see if it is willing to go with you.

✦ *statues of the mermaid goddesses*

✦ *models of fish, dolphins, crabs, etc.*

✦ *paintings or photos of mermaids*

✦ *some ocean water – or make your own brine by adding salt to water in an attractive container*

✦ *seaweed*

✦ *material with water patterns or fish-scales*

✦ *plants*

You can do the **Journey to your Inner Mermaid** (see page 20) and ask her what is needed. You can make special objects for your altar. You will know when your altar is ready by what it evokes in you. If you look at your altar and it oozes back at you the magic of mermaids then you are finished, for now.

Your Inner Mermaid incense burner

This is a terrific activity that can be done with a group (or school!) of your mermaid friends, either at an afternoon gathering or an evening party, or solo when you have a couple of hours free to yourself. Working with clay enhances everyone's creativity. And making a mermaid incense burner will not only provide you with a burner to use on a daily basis and to visit on your altar, but it will *also* connect you with your Inner Mermaid when you do the journey (guided meditation) before creating the piece. Multiple benefits! In today's busy world, who could ask for anything more!

WHAT YOU WILL NEED ...

✦ *self-hardening clay. This is the type of clay that does not need firing as it self-hardens. If you plan to create your incense burner in more than one sitting, you will need to keep it moist.*
✦ *a strong piece of cardboard to keep your burner on while it dries*

- ✦ *a good place to dry*
- ✦ *a working surface, which could be the cardboard and old newspapers*
- ✦ *a bowl of water*
- ✦ *old clothes or clothes that can get clay on them*
- ✦ *your journal*

Since your incense burner will reflect and resonate the energetic of your Inner Mermaid, it is time to go meet her! So put your materials aside because before you start creating your mermaid incense burner you are going to do your first journey in this book.

Journey to your Inner Mermaid

Find a time and a place when and where you will not be disturbed. If you have a cassette tape or CD of ocean sounds, put it on. Sit, stand or lie comfortably with your spine straight and close your eyes. Surround yourself with white light by envisioning yourself inside a luminous egg.

Breathe into your toes and as you exhale, tell your toes to relax. Breathe into your feet and ankles and as you exhale, tell your feet and ankles to relax. Breathe into your knees and thighs and as you exhale, tell your knees and thighs to relax. Breathe into your hips, buttocks and abdomen and as you exhale, tell your hips, buttocks and abdomen to relax. Breathe into your waist, chest and shoulders and as you exhale, tell your waist, chest and shoulders to relax. Breathe into your entire back and as you exhale, tell your entire back to relax. Breathe into your fingers and as you exhale, tell your fingers to relax. Breathe into your palms and wrists and as you exhale, tell you palms and wrists to relax. Breathe into your forearm and elbow and as you exhale, tell your forearm and elbow to relax. Breathe into your upper arm and as you exhale, tell your upper arm to relax. Breathe into your neck and as you exhale, tell your neck to relax. Breathe into your jaw and as you exhale, tell your jaw to relax. Breathe into your eyes and as you exhale, tell your eyes to relax. Breathe into your nose and sinuses and as you exhale, tell your nose and sinuses to relax. Breathe into your jaw, mouth and teeth and as you exhale, tell your jaw, mouth and teeth to relax. Breathe into your forehead and eyebrows and as you exhale, tell your forehead and eyebrows to relax. Breathe into your scalp and as you exhale, tell your scalp to relax.

Focus on your heart chakra which is located in the middle of your chest, near your heart. Breathe in and out of your heart chakra five times. Now see, sense or feel love. When you have got a fix on the quality of love, breathe love in and out of your heart chakra. If it helps you to visualize love as a white or coloured light, then do so. As you breathe love in, feel your heart chakra expand with love, like a balloon. When you exhale, feel the love circulating through your body. You may even want to send love to a particular area of your body.

While still breathing love in and out from your heart chakra, imagine yourself in front of your heart chakra. See, sense or feel your heart chakra as an enormous sacred well of swirling green water from the vantage point of a tiny, miniature version of you. Now dive into your heart chakra.

The green water feels soothing, loving and very joyful.

You are going down ... down, down, down ... deep into the core of your heart chakra. Down, down, down, feeling nurtured, comfortable and safe. Down, down, down, deeper and deeper and deeper, until you arrive at the core. There is a shimmering figure who meets you. She is glowing in her own radiance. She has the top half of a woman and the bottom half of a fish. You ask her who she is and she tells you her name and that she is your Inner Mermaid. You see clearly now what she looks like. Being with her feels very safe and fulfilling.

If you have any questions for her, you may ask them.

When you feel ready to return, you thank your Inner Mermaid for spending time with you. She thanks you for coming and tells you that she has been waiting for you to visit. She asks you for a gift and you give it to her with an open heart.

You begin swimming up, up, up, feeling refreshed, feeling nourished, feeling energized, up, up, up, feeling light, feeling loved, feeling revitalized, up, up, up, until your head breaks the surface of the well and you pull yourself out of the water, onto the side.

You take a deep breath and you are back breathing love in and out from your heart chakra. Focus on just breathing in and out from your heart chakra twice. Now take a deep breath and as you exhale, feel yourself back in your body. Take another deep breath and as you release it you are more present in your body and can move it gently. You take a last deep breath and as you exhale you may open your eyes.

Welcome back!

Take your journal and record your experience. Be sure to take the time you need. When you are finished writing, it is time to work with the clay. Please know that we were all endowed with abundant creativity at birth. Some of us have worked with our creativity so that the small flame we had at birth is now a large bonfire. Others have kept the fire burning low as a small ember. Whatever you have done with or thought about in the past regarding your creativity, you can always choose to do something different. One of the most important elements in making your incense burner and opening to the connection with your Inner Mermaid is allowing a sense of play and fun. A faithful, realistic rendition of your Inner Mermaid in clay is unnecessary. Know that whatever form you create will be absolutely what will serve you the best.

Now that you've created your incense burner you can use it in your daily rituals to help you connect with the mermaids.

Mermaid quickie

Here is a little quickie you can do to bring your Inner Mermaid into your daily routine. This works really well at the beginning of the day. I suggest setting a timer for 10–20 minutes so you'll remember to come out of the water and get on with your day!

1. Light a blue-green candle (like the ocean, if you can find it, or either a blue or green candle).

2. Light some incense in your incense burner – it could be a stick or cone or a leaf or twig or resin (it is up to you what you prefer). If you are scent sensitive, an excellent substitute to incense and the scent visceral is to use another sense: sound. I have been sounding smudging (smudging is when you cleanse a person's aura with something) people for ages. You can use chimes, drums, a bell, chant an OM, it is up to you.

3. Surround yourself with white light by envisioning yourself inside a luminous egg.

4. Close your eyes. Take a few deep inhalations and exhalations.

5. See, sense or feel yourself on a beach. Run into the ocean. The water is refreshingly joyful. As soon as you are submerged in the water, your legs transform into a tail. You are joined by your Inner Mermaid. You both swim together, leaping out of the water, generally frisking about. When you hear your alarm go off, thank your Inner Mermaid for coming and

run out of the water onto the beach and back into your body.

6. Take a deep breath, breathing in all the energy that was raised by your play.

7. Open your eyes and get on with your day!

Mermaid holiday

Holidays are so very vital to our health and well-being. They give us the necessary time away from our routine to shake out and shake up our energy and to come back to our lives reinvigorated. The next activity can be done anytime anywhere for a brief respite. It is designed to reset and refresh your internal computer and it costs nothing.

Putting on your mermaid glasses!

Imagine that right before you on a desk or table is a pair of glasses that enables you to see life through the eyes of a mermaid who has never before been on land. Take a deep breath and as you exhale, put on the glasses. You feel a switch being turned on in your brain. Now everything around you is extraordinary and marvellous. Completely different to anything you have ever seen before. Say to yourself:

'Everything is unique and wonderful.'

When you feel ready, take off the glasses. Be sure to remove the seaweed now dripping from your clothes!

Mermaid tea

When it comes to daily connection with mermaids, a terrific way of getting a good dose – and you may even decide to do it more – is to savour the connection while having a cup of tea!

In the spirit of getting more magic into your life, why not buzz your cup of tea with intent by learning how to charge the ingredients, thereby achieving twice the bang for your cuppa. In the following **Ritual for Charging Objects** (see page 30), you will focus on using empowering energy. At other times when you charge objects, you can choose other energies such as love, prosperity, finding a house, sex, and so on. Then when you drink or eat or wear the object, you will be filling yourself with that particular energy, which will help transform your life for the better.

INGREDIENTS

✦ *55g/2oz of whole kelp seaweed fronds packed into the measuring cup for the measure (digitata, also known as kombu, or kelp is usable)*
✦ *350ml/12oz cups spring water (or filtered water)*
✦ *1 tea bag of organic green tea*

As discussed in the Introduction, these ingredients can be found in most local health food stores, or you may check the Resource Guide at the end of the book for details on how to purchase them on-line. Remember to buy organic if you can!

Ritual for charging objects

1. Light a candle.
2. Surround yourself with white light by envisioning yourself inside a luminous egg.
3. Focus on your heart chakra. Breathe in and out of your heart chakra five times. Now see, sense or feel love. Focus on the quality of love and breathe love in and out of your heart chakra.
4. Focus on your Inner Mermaid and establish contact by seeing, feeling or sensing her presence.
5. Ask her if she is willing to flow the empowering energy of the mermaids through you. When she agrees, continue.
6. Take the seaweed and the green tea into your hands and hold them to your heart.
7. Feel the empowering mermaid energy build up in your heart.
8. When there is a strong build up of energy, will the empowering mermaid energy into the seaweed and tea bag in your hands.

9. Feel, sense or see the objects you are holding become charged with energy.

10. Take a deep breath and as you exhale stop the flow of energy.

11. Give thanks to your Inner Mermaid.

12. Focus on breathing love in and out of your heart chakra.

13. Blow out the candle.

14. If you feel a strong build up of energy in your body, you can place your hands on the ground and give it back to the earth.

Making your mermaid tea

Now that your ingredients are powered up it is time to go ahead and make the tea. The recipe is for one cup, but you may make a litre of the seaweed broth at a time and keep it in the refrigerator, then heat up enough for a cup of tea.

1. Place the seaweed in a stainless steel saucepan and add the water and cover. Bring to a boil and then simmer for 30 minutes.
2. While the kelp is simmering, be sure to breathe in deep the smell of the sea!
3. Strain the liquid into a cup and add the green tea bag. Keep bag in according to your taste.
4. As you drink your mermaid tea, savour the taste of the sea and feel the energy of mermaid empowerment flooding your being.

De-stressing with the mermaids

We all know that stress is a killer. Stress eats away at our health by disrupting our immune system. Stress pressure cooks our psychological balance and tips us over into anxiety and panic. Stress re-tailors the good fit of our relationships into baggy pants and shrunken tops. The bad news about stress is that in our fast-paced twenty-first century life, it is here to stay. The good news is there are ways we can choose to cope with it that can bring us many blessings. One of the 'blessings' is that we get to meet our first mermaid goddess, **Hina Lau Limu Kala** in a Mythological Moment before we experience her seaweed de-stressor.

Mythological Moment:
Hina Lau Limu Kala

The Polynesian Great Goddess Hina is an all embracing concept that has many facets. It is said that the term 'Hina' means a personification of the feminine creative and manifesting force, which is why there are so many Hinas in the mythology of islands populated by Polynesians. In Hawaii, when Hina Lau Limu Kala is spoken of it is Hina in her mermaid aspect: she who governs the kahunas (indigenous shamans) who heal with medicines from the sea and first ancestress from whom all Hawaiians descend. She is also known to appear in the form of limu kala seaweed - hence her name.

Of the many myths about her, the most well-known is when she was a mortal woman living on earth. One day while bathing in a secret, hidden pool, she was made love to by a very attractive eel. When her relatives found out, they grew fearful and destroyed the eel, who happened to be a god. Resourceful Hina took the head of her lover and buried it in the sand. Thus was born the first coconut tree.

Like all Hinas, Hina loves music and dancing the Hula, which is a traditional dance of shaman-priestesses in honour of their Goddesses. Hina is happy to assist you with healing and work-related issues.

Journey to Hina

Find a time and a place when and where you will not be disturbed. Sit, lie or stand with your spine straight and close your eyes. Take a deep breath and release it with a sigh. Take another deep breath and release it with a moan. Take a last deep breath and release it with a snake-like hiss. Let your breathing return to normal.

See, sense or feel the entrance to a cave. It can be a cave that you know or one that exists in your imagination. Take a deep breath and as you exhale, stand at the mouth of the cave. Put your hand on the cave's opening. What does it feel like? Now enter the cave.

The cave is a good size, comfortably warm and well lit. You walk to the back of the cave and notice that it becomes a tunnel. You enter the tunnel and go down, down, down. Deeper and deeper and deeper. Down, down, down. Becoming more relaxed, letting go, going deeper. Down, down, down. Deeper and deeper and deeper. Until you reach the end where you see some different coloured light. On the count of three you will step out into the otherworld. One – two – three. Step out of the tunnel.

You are on one of the most beautiful beaches in the world. Clean, white, soft sand and dazzling blue ocean. You sit on the beach and watch the waves. They are enormous and quite powerful and they beat upon the beach as if on a drum. As you observe the ocean you notice that it is growing calmer and calmer and calmer, until the waves are mere ripples on the surface of the sea. You now notice a large clump of brown seaweed which has come in with the tide.

Slowly you watch as the seaweed begins to rise, move about, then leap into the air. Once in the air it transforms into a mermaid with long black hair and a silver-blue fish-tail that dives back into the sea. It is Hina and she waves to you, gesturing for you to join her in the sea. You get up and walk to the ocean, slowly entering the warm almost bath-like water. Hina swims over and greets you with an engaging smile.

She tells you that you look like you have too much stress in your life and tells you she has the solution, if you are willing to trust her. You say yes and she tells you to float. You lie on your back and surrender to the movement of the ocean. Hina puts her hands under you and when you feel her touch, you relax and let go even more. There is nothing but being in this moment with the smell of the sea, the pulse of the water, the feeling of the sun gently warming your skin.

You hear a deep, low base tone and Hina's voice explaining that you are going to shape-shift (change your outward form) into a large clump of seaweed; she will change into seaweed with you. As you hear the tone again, you feel yourself slowly shrinking as you begin to transform into seaweed. Parts of you contract into stem as other parts of you expand into long thin fronds. It is dramatically different from anything you have ever experienced before. You feel lighter and simpler. The sun on your leaves is a new sensation.

It is an amazing feeling to be a bunch of seaweed floating in the Pacific ocean. You respond to every pulse, every nuance of the sea. The wind blows and you move. The sea breathes and you move. You drift weightlessly on the top of the ocean. Weightless, boneless, nervous system-less. You feel completely relaxed. It is very deeply peaceful and refreshing. And you drift, the sun's rays soaking into your cells.

After an amount of time that is appropriate for you, you hear Hina telling you it is time to return. When you hear the low deep base tone you feel yourself begin to grow back into your usual form. You feel your bones again and skin, everything that makes you a human being. Hina is before you laughing with merriment, and you, feeling light and buoyant, laugh with her. You thank Hina for her seaweed secrets and she gives you a hug.

You emerge from the ocean, feeling calm, at peace and still floating. You easily find the opening of the tunnel and you enter.

Now you are going up, up, up, feeling clear and clean, refreshed and revitalized, up, up, up, with a deepening sense of peace, lots of space and quiet within, up, up, up, awake and aware, till you re-enter the cave. You walk out of the mouth of the cave and take a deep breath. As you release it you are back in your body. You take another deep breath and as you release it you are more present in your body and can move it gently. You take a last deep breath and as you exhale you may open your eyes.

Welcome back!

Now take your journal and record your experience.

This is a wonderful way to prepare for any magic that you will create. It is vitally important to be clear and clean emotionally and mentally before engaging in any rituals. This is why wise-women healers of old, those known as witches, would use a broom to sweep their spaces prior to any working of magic. While they swept their physical-tangible-everyday space, they were clearing and cleaning their inner space or their mental and emotional bodies.

Acquiring your mermaid tail

One absolute fun essential for your mermaid wardrobe is your own mermaid's tail. Your tail is something you might want to wear to parties, or use when you go out and about – while carried in the arms of your devotees, of course. Just remember not to let any man steal it or you may be forced to become his wife, till you get it back!

As mermaids-in-training, if our magic isn't strong enough yet to make or grow our own tail, this is a wonderful substitute. If you are rich in sewing magic, the whole wild world of fabric is at your fingertips. Use the following as a springboard for your own expertise. For those whose abilities don't include skill with a needle or sewing machine, these instructions are for you. Yet another way to get hold of a tail would be to hire a competent tailor or seamstress to make you one, or trade skills with a friend, or check the back of this book in the Resource Guide and commission a tail from a tail-maker! And remember, in today's high-tech world, if all else fails, there's always the stapler.

We're going to go for a tight-fitting tail that you pull on, like a pair of trousers. You can purchase material that looks 'fishy' or buy a solid colour that works for you. Although these instructions are for hand-painting or drawing scales on your piece of material with a fabric marker or paint, you may elect to purchase fabric in different shimmery colours and cut out scales and sew them on.

Where do your feet go? Right, you can make the end of the tail in a large piece of white muslin, big enough to fit your feet into, and then paint it to look 'finny', and stuff it with pillow-stuffing material so it looks like a big fin and hides your feet. Or you can use more of the 2-way stretch fabric you use for the body of the tail.

WHAT YOU WILL NEED ...

✦ *2-way stretch fabric – when you measure at your local fabric store, you will need enough to wrap around your hips, where the tail will start, down to your ankles, and then enough to cover your feet and make a big fin.*

✦ *white muslin – enough to cover your feet and make a big fin (if not using the 2-way stretch fabric)*

✦ *fabric paints or markers in iridescent colours, or day glo, or whatever goes with your tail-design concept*

✦ *pillow stuffing or quilt batting*

✦ *thread*

ASSEMBLING YOUR MERMAID TAIL

1. Put on your favourite energizing music.

2. With the fabric on the wrong side, sew together your fabric so that it is a tube that is wide at one end and narrow at the other, and that fits you around your hips and smoothly fits the rest of your body.

3. Draw the size of the fin on the muslin; be sure to make it an inch or two larger. Cut it out and sew the wrong sides together.

4. Paint or draw scales all over on the right side of your tail body and let dry.

5. Paint the right side of the entire muslin fin and let dry. Stuff the fin.

6. Sew the top of the fin to the body of the tail. You may want to add more paint so that you can't see the seam and that it all blends together.

7. Put on your tail and admire yourself in the mirror.

8. Take yourself out to a fabulous fish dinner!

If you are wondering what to wear with your tail on top, depending on what circles you frequent, you can go *au naturale* (nude) or take a bra top or bathing suit top and attach shells, beads and/or glittery stones with a hot glue gun. Now you are ready to consort with the mermaids as an equal. No longer a tailless wannabe. Enjoy!

Mermaid Interlude: Mermaid's Vengeance

The following story comes from Robert Hunt, who edited a group of tales from Cornwall, the West of England, in 1903, of which he said, 'Several versions of the following story have been given me. The general idea of the tale belongs to the north coast; but the fact of mermaidens taking innocents under their charge was common around the Lizard, and in some of the coves near the Land's End.'[8]

A poor but hard-working couple had a daughter upon whom they doted. Her father, Penna, worked for the local Squire, with whom he was a great favourite. Alas, because of the Squire's great preference for his worker, his overseer, Chenalls, was jealous and detested him, doing everything he could to make Penna's life miserable. The only joy the diligent and honourable Penna had was the time he spent with his daughter, Selina, taking long walks by the sea.

Selina, at eighteen, combined

the endowments of a well-developed woman with the fresh innocence and purity of a child. Many in the village argued that she was a changeling, for her mother, Honour, had bathed her since the time of her birth in the same rocky pool along the shore that mermaids were known to use. Others were content to say that she was a very pretty girl and leave it at that.

The Squire had a nephew, Walter Trewoofe, a young soldier, who was a very dissolute, handsome and proud young man and of whom he was very fond. He was always paying Walter's gambling debts and getting him out of trouble, trusting that it was just the wildness of youth and that he would come to his senses and settle down as he grew older. Walter had recently fought in a war and had returned to his uncle to recover his health.

Chenalls knew of Penna's love for his daughter and with the arrival of young Walter, decided to use Selina to destroy her father. First he wormed his way into the confidences of Walter by making himself indispensable. Seeing that Walter had a fondness for strong drink and debauchery, and a mind that viewed women only as whores, he baited Walter with Selina, telling him lies about the girl. Soon Walter was seen out walking with Selina and her father.

Walter didn't need much encouragement to woo Selina. He was delighted with her above average beauty. He flattered and charmed her mother, too. Simple child-like Selina soon fell in love with the sophisticated, worldly and experienced Walter. She had been brought up to trust and she trusted him completely and believed that he loved her, too. Her mother had high hopes of a marriage, which would raise the status of the family. Whenever Selina was with Walter, he declared his love for her. He won through her resolve by appealing to her heart. She opened herself to him completely and gave him access to her total being. He told her to keep their love a secret for now, because he was trying to get his uncle's permission to marry her. Not a word. Even to her father.

Next Chenalls arranged for Penna to be transferred to a distant farm, where he could get home only once in a three-month period. Penna's visit confirmed that his relationship with his daughter had changed. Something felt dreadfully wrong. It wrung his heart to have to go back to his job. His daughter didn't seem like the same person he had known since her birth. She held herself back and wouldn't tell him what was happening.

During this time many of the village noticed an increase in mermaid sightings that seemed to time itself to when Selina and Walter walked by the sea. Others dismissed the talk as the imaginings of the fanciful.

Another three months passed and Walter left town one day, without a word to anyone, except his uncle. Selina, beside herself with grief at the sudden loss of her lover, withdrew into herself and spent her days sorrowing alone in her darkened room. Not even the presence of her father, now permitted to return home by Chenalls once the damage was done, could console her.

With perfect timing Chenalls chose his moment to strike: he taunted Penna about using his daughter's virginity to secure his family's rise in estate and was rewarded with a blow to the head. This is what he had been waiting for. Chenalls immediately went to the Squire and told him that Penna's daughter Selina had seduced an innocent Walter and now the family were hoping to benefit financially through redress of a non-existent wrong.

The Squire questioned some of the villagers. Hoping to get on Chenalls' good side, these folks backed up his story. Penna was dismissed from the Squire's service and the family had to vacate their home on his land. Being such a good worker, Penna landed another situation and the family obtained a new home.

Selina, however, did not recover from her betrayal. Daily she grew weaker and weaker. She was heard during this time, to communicate with beings that her mother and father could not see, but whose presence they felt. These conversations brought Selina some peace; however, they weren't enough to keep her in this life and she soon departed leaving a newborn babe behind.

When Selina died, Chenalls' life fell apart. Cattle died, crops failed, hay stacks caught on fire.

Chenalls began drinking heavily which rendered him unfit for his job. Not even Walter's appeal to his uncle, upon his return to his uncle's estate, could help. Chenalls bought a cottage on a cliff which now became a local hang-out for wild young men and women. Goings on at the cottage were rough, violent and fuelled by excessive drink. Walter was a regular there.

One night while heading home, Walter missed his usual path and found himself wandering by the sea. He heard an ethereal sad song and followed it to its source:

> 'The stars are beautiful, when bright
> They are mirror'd in the sea;
> But they are pale beside that light
> Which was so beautiful to me.
> My angel child, my earth-born girl,
> From all your kindred riven,
> By the base deeds of a selfish churl,
> And to a sand-grave driven!
> How shall I win thee back to ocean?
> How canst thou quit thy grave,

To share again the sweet emotion
Of gliding through the wave?"[9]

Sitting on a rock by the mouth of a cavern he beheld the most beautiful woman he had ever seen. She didn't seem to notice him until she had finished her song and then she looked over at him and shrieked. He sprang on her and grabbed her arm, twisting it behind her back saying, 'I'll not let you go yet, my lovely songbird.' It was then that he saw her face as she turned and looked him full in the eye. She was an exact replica of the loving face of Selina, except for a fierce power that he couldn't withstand. He instantly froze in her gaze and numbly dropped her arm, unable to move or speak. Then she spoke to him:

'Go to the grave where the sinless one sleepeth!
Bring her cold corpse where her guarding one
weepeth.
Look on her, love her again, ay! Betray her,
And wreath with false smiles the
pale face of her slayer!

Go go! Now, and feel the full force of my sorrow!
For the glut of my vengeance there cometh a morrow.'[10]

When morning came, the sea reaching out to touch his feet brought him out of his state. The maiden was gone and though he called after her and looked for her, she could not be found.

Walter Trewoofe returned home a changed man. There was now this looming sense of guilt and wretchedness that shot through his life. He couldn't eat without thinking of she he had wronged. He couldn't sleep without remembering how he had betrayed her. Finally he sought out her grave and there, watered it with his tears. Chenalls and his old friends hunted him down and brought him to the cottage. Try as he might, he could find no enjoyment in his former habits. It seemed that something was keeping him in check. Some invisible power. The more he tried to take up his former life, the more exhausted and weak he felt, until he lost his health completely.

All he could see before him was the beautiful face of the woman who looked like Selina. He had fallen in love with her and was now lost in pining. Finally he could take it no longer and resolved to seek her out, even though there was a goodly amount of fear mixed in with the love. He went to the cavern where he had first met her. A celebratory song filled the air from the same magical voice:

> *'Join all hands–*
> *Might and main,*
> *Weave the sands,*
> *Form a chain,*
> *He, my lover,*
> *Comes again!*

> *From your couch of glistening pearl,*
> *Slowly, softly, come away;*
> *Our sweet earth-child, lovely girl,*
> *Died this day, – died this day.'*[11]

As he walked towards the being who sang the joyful song, he remembered that Selina had died a year ago. The singer stood and welcomed him with a voice that sounded like Selina's. She invited him to sit next to her, which he did.

'Did you love her, Selina?' asked the maiden.

'Yes', replied Walter.

'Then I shall love you as you have loved her,' and then she took his head in her hands and kissed him on the lips. He felt his breath die and his lungs freeze. 'Kisses are different for sea folk than they are for land folk. The kiss of a mermaid is an unbreakable bond. We are united until your death.'

'My death', stammered Walter, 'what do you mean by my death?'

But the maiden said nothing. She merely continued to treat him as he had treated Selina. All the words he used to woo her, he heard now from his companion. All the false smiles, flattery, gooey murmurings, all was visited upon him. Finally the torment grew so great that he could no longer bear it.

'Please let me go, I'll do anything you say,' he begged. 'Please forgive me. You are right, I used and betrayed her. I am responsible for her death.'

'Bring me Selina, alive,' replied the maiden, 'otherwise you are mine to do with as I please.'

The sound of thunder was heard, lightning cracked the night sky. The waves were now pouring over them as the storm struck them in the face full force. As the water rose higher, the maiden took Walter to higher points on the rocks. Now the waves were beating in a tumultuous roar against the cliff. Walter looked on with horror as a lightning bolt struck Chenalls' cottage and exploded it into flames. Soon all the waves were alive with mermaids and they lifted him up and tossed him about on the sea as they sang:

'Come away, come away,
O'er the waters wild!
Our earth-born child
Died this day, died this day.

'Come away, come away!
The tempest loud
Weaves the shroud
For him who did betray.

'Come away, come away!
Beneath the wave
Lieth the grave
Of him we slay, him we slay.

'Come away, come away!
He shall not rest
In earth's own breast
For many a day, many a day.

'Come away, come away!
By billows to roast
From coast to coast,
Like deserted boat
His corpse shall float
Around the bay, around the bay.'[12]

Lunar magic

This brings us on to lunar magic. The moon is the planet you want to work with for mermaid magic because the moon rules the ocean's tides, affects our emotional bodies and ourselves, and represents the feminine in our astrological charts.

Lunar magic is a conscious partnership between you and the moon. You use the cycles of the moon and what they represent, as well as what astrological sign the moon is in to do magic. **By use of 'magic' I mean your focused intent**. As you know, there are twelve astrological signs and they are: Aries, Taurus, Gemini, Cancer, Leo, Virgo, Libra, Scorpio, Sagittarius, Capricorn, Aquarius, Pisces. All you will need to do lunar magic is have a clear intent for what you want to create with your magic and a calendar with the phases of the moon along with a listing of when the moon is in what sign.

Although the moon has sixteen phases to her cycles of waxing and waning, for our purpose in creating lunar magic we will be using the rhythms of increase and decrease. The full moon is the strongest point in the cycle of increase and the new moon or dark of the moon is the time of the strongest point of decrease.

Simply speaking, when you want something to increase in your life, the time to do a ritual and create magic is as the moon is waxing: from the time you notice the crescent moon after the dark moon on your calendar or in the sky till the time of the full moon. If you want something to decrease in your life, then the time to do a ritual and create magic is when the moon is waning: from the time after the full moon and you see a less than full circle on your calendar or in the sky till the time of the dark of the moon. An example would be doing a ritual for bringing love into your life during the time leading up to the full moon. Another example would be doing a ritual for removing obstacles to your calling in the best romantic partner, or becoming financially abundant, at the time leading up to the dark of the moon.

For a breakdown of which mermaid to work with when the moon is in a particular sign, please see the Appendix at the back of the book. These are suggestions based on my experience. You are developing your own relationship with the mermaids, and if you need to do a particular ritual at a time that deviates from my suggestion, check in with your Inner Mermaid, and if she gives you the green light, go ahead. Likewise for following my list about who to work with when. You may have such a tight relationship with the mermaid goddess Yemanja (who we will be meeting in the following chapter), for example, that you may want to call on her for everything! The best magic happens when you follow your own inner guidance and do what feels right to you.

By aligning yourself with the moon's cycles you are giving yourself a lovely treat. One way to get the most from lunar magic is to journal your experiences with the moon at its different phases.

Now we have learnt how to contact the mermaids and are comfortable working with some tools and techniques, we will move on to the sweet mystery of love.

CHAPTER 3

Mermaid Magic for Love and Sex

To me the words of the Beatles say it all: 'All you need is love' and 'Love is all there is.' So profound, so sixties, so true. Life begins with love, the joyous and ecstatic act of 'making love', so that is where we shall begin.

In this chapter we will swim into the deeper waters of love, self-healing, sexuality, romance and relationships with the mermaids as our guides and teachers. With their joyful assistance, we will be able to move smoothly and easily through these realms, and have a whale of a great time, too.

Self-healing with the mermaids

The universe we live in vibrates to the key of love. In order to attend the wonderfully delicious love party that life is, especially from a 'mer' perspective, we must first create our invite by healing ourselves so we can resonate at that nourishing frequency. All of us who have been wounded in the dance of life have spaces inside us of dark held energy. Think of it as inner scars. These spaces take up space and keep us from filling completely with love. When we heal our woundings, those places of held dark energy are freed and opened up, and can now be used for the high, blissful energy of love. As we have noticed from the previous rituals we have done, we must first raise our energy to the vibration of love in order to connect with the mermaids and make mermaid magic.

Since magic is made from ourselves, from all of who we are, if we are walking around with wounds the size of soccer stadiums, it would be prudent to do some self-healing. Part of the package we accept with human incarnation is that our greatest teachers are our wounds. The conscious decision to accept and heal those wounds brings about our empowerment and joy. It will also make it easier for the mermaids to connect with us.

There is no better mermaid goddess to call upon for self-healing than that great ocean mother herself, **Yemanja**.

Mythological Moment: Yemanja

Ocean Mother of the Yoruban pantheon of gods is a West African creator deity who also gave birth to all the waters and all that lives in them. Yemanja accompanied her human children when they came to be sold as slaves in North America, Brazil, Haiti, Cuba and the Caribbean, hence the different spellings of her name.

Although Yemanja is considered a maternal goddess, answering prayers for fertility, pregnancy and childbirth, she loves to help out in affairs of the heart. She is also fantastic with anything requiring abundance, and is the mermaid goddess contacted by those who make a living from the sea. It is wise to ask permission before taking anything from Her kingdom, as she can be wrathful to those who take her other children, the fish, out of her waters. Her colours are blue, white and silver and she is associated with the number seven. Her days of worship include June 22, September 7 and 9, October 26, December 31, January 1 and February 2. She loves offerings of flowers.

Yemanja appeared as Herself in a supporting role in the movie *Woman on Top* (2000) about a Brazilian chef, played by Penelope Cruz, who finds, loses and finds her love again with the help of Yemanja. The filmmakers did a wonderful job of evoking Her energy.

Yemanja is a very alive and active mermaid Goddess, and is worshipped yearly on February 2, in Salvador da Bahia, northeastern Brazil, with a huge ceremony-festival of hundreds of people dressed in white, singing, dancing, making music and processing with their offerings to where the sand meets the sea. This is the time of year when Yemanja is thanked for her bounty and appealed to for further abundance for the next year.

Now we are ready for our visit with Yemanja, because no matter how old or young or what stage or state of life we are in, we could always use a bit of 'mothering' to help us heal our wounds.

Journey to Yemanja

Find a time and a place when and where you will not be disturbed. Light a blue or white candle. Next light a stick, cone, twig or leaf (whichever you prefer) of incense in your incense burner, or if you are scent sensitive, use sound and ring a bell or use a chime, or chant an OM. Now surround yourself with white light. As you know, this can be visualized as an iridescent white oval, like an egg, encompassing your entire body. You are now ready for your **Journey to Yemanja**.

Sit, lie or stand with your spine straight and close your eyes. Take a deep breath and release it with a sigh. Take another deep breath and release it with a moan. Take a last deep breath and release it with a snake-like hiss. Let your breathing return to normal.

See, sense or feel the entrance to a cave. It can be a cave that you know or one that exists in your imagination. Take a deep breath and as you exhale, stand at the mouth of the cave. Put your hand on the cave's opening. What does it feel like? Now enter the cave.

The cave is a good size, comfortably warm and well lit. You walk to the back of the cave and notice that it becomes a tunnel. You enter the tunnel and go down, down, down. Deeper and deeper and deeper. Down, down, down. Becoming more relaxed, letting go, going deeper. Down, down, down. Deeper and deeper and deeper. Until you reach the end where you see some different coloured light. On the count of three you will step out into the otherworld. One – two – three. Step out of the tunnel.

You are on a natural beach with soft fine sand and palm trees. It is warm and you walk down to the ocean. You let the tiny waves lick your feet and legs. The water is the perfect temperature for you. You look at the expanse of sea and you notice a beautiful woman with rich, luxuriant and gleaming ebony skin and hair, regal and queenly, dressed in blue, white and silver, rising out of the water. It is Yemanja. When she tells you to come and join her, you swim out to her.

She looks at you closely with deep compassionate eyes and you feel yourself melting into her. As you both gaze into each other's eyes, she dissolves into the ocean inviting you to surrender to her and let her hold you. Gently and carefully, you feel Yemanja's embrace and you let it in. You feel her pouring love into you, holding you, comforting you, caring for you. And you do whatever is appropriate for you. You give over and allow yourself to be held by the Mother. You feel her heartbeat, the rhythm of the sea. You smell her scent – salt water. You feel her capacity to be fully present as she holds you. You continue in Yemanja's embrace for as long as is needed.

Yemanja and you both release from your contact at the same time. She re-materializes beside you, and you thank her. She asks you for something and you give it with an open heart. You bid each other good-bye and you turn, easily finding the opening of the tunnel which you enter.

Now you are going up, up, up, feeling clear and clean, refreshed and revitalized, up, up, up, with a deepening sense of peace, lots of space and quiet within, up, up, up, awake and aware, till you re-enter the cave. You walk out of the mouth of the cave and take a deep breath. As you release it you are back in your body. You take another deep breath and as you release it you are more present in your body and can move it gently. You take a last deep breath and as you exhale you may open your eyes.

Welcome back!

Blow out the candle and record your experience in your journal.

Mermaid secrets for self-love

A vital ingredient in your ability to manifest love in your life is how much you are able to love yourself. By this I mean you can only give what you have and you can't give what you don't have. Being able to love yourself fully and unconditionally will make you a homing device for love. It will etherically float an 'eat here now' sign above your head.

There are so many scrumptious ways to love ourselves, thanks to the assistance of the mermaids! Ways that are sensuous delights. Like the following!

Mermaid bath and self-love ritual

YOU WILL NEED ...

+ *225g/8oz digitata (also known as kombu) seaweed*
+ *225g/8oz bladderwrack seaweed*
+ *115g/4oz Irish moss seaweed*
+ *4 litres/135oz spring water (or filtered water)*
+ *cheesecloth*
+ *a handheld mirror*
+ *pink candle*
+ *incense and incense burner*
+ *tape or CD of ocean sounds (optional)*

MERMAID BATH-TIME!

1. Pour 4 litres of spring or filtered water into a stainless steel pot, put the lid on and bring to a boil.
2. Mix the seaweeds in a bowl.
3. Cut 2 pieces of cheesecloth 30 × 30cm/1 × 1ft and place them on top of each other, so that you have doubled the thickness of the cheesecloth.

4. If you have a tape or CD of ocean sounds, bring it into the bathroom to play during your bath.

5. Pour the seaweeds into the centre of the cheesecloth and tie it up with string to make a bag.

6. Now add the cheesecloth bag to the pot of boiling water and let it sit unheated while you run a hot bath. When the bath is almost full, turn off the water and add the contents of the pot to the bath. Check the temperature. If it is too hot for you to enter, wait until the bath cools down to your taste, then enter.

7. Set a hand mirror next to the bath.

8. Light a pink candle and bring some incense in your burner into the bathroom. Ignite the incense, inviting in the presence and assistance of your Inner Mermaid. The best way to establish contact is by seeing, feeling or sensing her presence.

9. Surround yourself with white light by envisioning yourself inside a luminous egg.

10. Enter your bath, if the temperature of your bath water is ready for you, inhaling deeply the seaweed aroma – the ocean's perfume.

11. Rub the cheesecloth bag over your body and fully enjoy the sensual experience. Breathe into your body and give thanks for its beauty and perfection! That's right, it is beautiful and perfect no matter what you think of it!

12. Gaze at yourself in the mirror and say '*I love you*, _____'(your name). And let that soak in. Really maintain eye contact with yourself and speak directly and lovingly to the person you see looking out at you in the mirror. Keep doing this until you feel it (that could be about five minutes).

13. Rub the cheesecloth bag over your body, until the seaweed is no longer gelatinous.

14. Thank your Inner Mermaid and blow out the candle to end your ritual.

15. Total time you will want to spend in the bath is roughly 30 minutes. You may need to add more hot water.

16. If you begin to grow a fish tail, don't panic! Just joking!

Your bath is your place to revert to your wild primal self. Like Melusine, who made her husband swear that he would not look in on her on Saturdays, mermaids who live on land need to spend time in their bath regenerating. The bath will do wonders for your skin and the self-love will leave you feeling calm and juicy! This is a good ritual to incorporate into your life once a week. You can, of course, make use of your mirror any time, giving yourself five minutes of self-love daily.

Connecting with your soul

Continuing on our path to manifesting love and sex in our life, we will visit the Emerald Isle for an introduction to the mermaid goddess **Liban**, who will then help us connect with our soul, our own piece of Divine love and light within.

The soul is the place where the blueprint for this lifetime is stored. The soul therefore affects our love life, our work life; in fact, everything. Connection with our soul brings us the knowledge we need to align with our soul's plan and helps ease our way. The benefit of choosing to live the voice of our soul brings peace, serenity and the blessings of a joyous life.

Mythological Moment: Liban

Liban, the merrow, or mermaid goddess, hails from Ireland. Some legends say she was originally a human who drowned and was transformed into a mermaid. She became a sanctified mermaid (the only one I've ever read about) because she petitioned St. Comgall to help grant her a soul. Other legends tell of a sacred healing well and an arrogant woman who didn't give the well its due respect. In rage the well overflowed, drowning the entire village, which included Liban and her dog. And yet others say she is the daughter of the Irish god, Eochaid, who ran off with his stepmother. Liban and her lapdog were the only ones who survived the flood sent to his household by the angry gods in vengeance for Eochaid's flagrance.

For hundreds of years Liban lived in the depths of the sea, she in the shape of a salmon, a fish of knowledge and wisdom to the Celts, and her dog as an otter. Curious about what was happening on land, Liban transformed herself into a mermaid and allowed herself to be caught with her faithful otter friend. While the both of them were being exhibited as a curiosity, a vicious, depraved man killed the otter. Out of grief for the loss of her animal companion, Liban changed into a human and died.

Liban is a lover of animals, a virgin (and here virgin means whole unto herself without a consort or partner), and capable of connecting to her deepest most spiritual parts.

We are now ready to meet with Liban, learn her ways of wisdom and gain her assistance in connecting with our soul.

Journey to Liban

Find a time and a place when and where you will not be disturbed. Sit, lie or stand with your spine straight and close your eyes. Surround yourself with white light by envisioning yourself inside a luminous egg. Now take a deep breath and release it with a sigh. Take another deep breath and release it with a moan. Take a last deep breath and release it with a snake-like hiss. Let your breathing return to normal.

See, sense or feel the entrance to a cave. It can be a cave that you know or one that exists in your imagination. Take a deep breath and as you exhale, stand at the mouth of the cave. Put your hand on the cave's opening. What does it feel like? Now enter the cave.

The cave is a good size, comfortably warm and well lit. You walk to the back of the cave and notice that it becomes a tunnel. You enter the tunnel and go down, down, down. Deeper and deeper and deeper. Down, down, down. Becoming more relaxed, letting go, going deeper. Down, down, down. Deeper and deeper and deeper. Until you reach the end where you see some different coloured light. On the count of three you will step out into the otherworld. One – two – three. Step out of the tunnel.

You are standing on the shore of a brilliantly clear blue lake, Lough Neagh, and you hear the barking of a small dog, who runs up to you. The dog barks at you indicating that you are to follow him. He runs into the water and when his whole body is submerged in the lake, he changes into an otter. You follow him and when you dive into the lake you are transformed into a mermaid with a salmon's tail. You can breathe under the water, too.

You follow the otter into the middle of the lake where there is a castle and swim through an open window. Once inside the castle the otter leads you to a beautiful suite of rooms where Liban is waiting for you. You feel a deep sense of healing in her presence, as if all the cares and woes of your life had just been lifted off you. She smiles at you and tells you you can always have your cares and woes back; she will keep them safe for you while you are here with her.

Liban invites you to come and sit in front of her in a richly cushioned chair. You do so and now you are both sitting facing each other. Liban asks if she may take your hands. You say yes and she takes your hands in hers.

You feel an electric current, strong and soothing, begin to run through your body, and hear a low hum. You sit there allowing the current with its penetrating hum to run through you and find yourself continually opening to it. At each point of opening, you feel an even deeper sense of peace and tranquillity. After each point of opening you notice a higher and finer connection with your most authentic piece, your soul. Finally, you discover that the current has opened you up on your deepest levels and assisted you in connecting with your soul. You feel completely whole and centred in the core of your being. Joyful and free, you have come home to yourself.

Your soul tells you that you are deeply loved, accepted and cherished. That you are the beloved of your soul. Your soul relates that she is connected to the source, the Divine, and that by connecting with her you will experience that deep love, peace, inner blessing and sense of fulfilment.

When you have had your fill of this experience, you thank Liban for her gift. She thanks you and you both disengage hands. The otter appears and you follow him out of the castle and back to the shore of the lake. As soon as your upper body is out of the water, you transform back into your original form. You easily find the opening of the tunnel and you enter.

Now you are going up, up, up, feeling clear and clean, refreshed and revitalized, up, up, up, with a deepening sense of peace, and lots of space and quiet within, up, up, up, awake and aware, till you re-enter the cave. You walk out of the mouth of the cave and take a deep breath. As you release it you are back in your body. You take another deep breath and as you release it you are more present in your body and can move it gently. You take a last deep breath and as you exhale you may open your eyes.

Welcome back! Now journal your experience.

Mermaid Interlude: Undine

Now we visit medieval Germany for the story of Undine. Undines are water elementals, or spirits. They are also mermaids and they can take any form they wish. The following is crafted from a mixture of Undine stories, including Jean Giraudoux's play, *Ondine* (which starred Audrey Hepburn in 1954) and Friedrich de la Motte Fouque's *Undine*, published in 1867.

A fisherman and his wife gave birth to a daughter in the autumn years of their life. One day when the husband was out fishing, his wife was playing with their daughter, now three years old, on a rock overlooking a deep lake that was not far from their humble home. Suddenly the daughter, who was in her mother's lap, wriggled free from her embrace, dove into the lake and immediately vanished. The distraught mother called out for her child, ran around the lake trying to find her, all to no avail. The little girl had disappeared. There was nothing for the mother to do but to grieve, break the sad news to her husband and grieve some more.

They were deep in their sorrow that night when they heard a knock at their door. Since they lived all alone next to an enchanted forest, and had no visitors, ever, imagine their surprise when they opened the door and there was a little girl of about three with hair like spun gold, richly dressed in garments befitting a princess. When asked where her parents were, the little one pointed at the lake. When asked what her name was, she told them Undine. What could they do but adopt her then and there.

Fifteen years passed and then one night in a particularly tempestuous rain storm, a knight errant appeared at their cottage asking for food and shelter. The old couple made him at home with food and drink and sat him by the fire to hear his story. He told them he was Sir Hans of Ringstetten, his ancestral home was a castle near the Danube and that for love of the Princess Bertha, he had braved the enchanted forest. She had sent him on this errand for proof of his love for her. They told him their story and about their foster-daughter, Undine, who was not quite like other women and who liked to be near water, almost all of the time.

At that moment, the door of the cottage flew open and Undine appeared. Did I say that she was gorgeous? Possessing an ethereal and sensual beauty not of this world? Did I mention how handsome the knight was? Dare I tell you that they both marvelled at the beauty of the other and fell instantly and deeply in love with each other? Well they did. So much so that all thoughts of Bertha – and the fisherman, in all fairness to the knight, did bring her up several times – were gone. 'It was, it is, it will ever be Undine,' was what Sir Hans now said. 'I never knew love till I saw Undine,' was what Sir Hans explained. And that was that.

Undine was wildly happy that night. She was certain that Sir Hans loved her. After all he had asked her to marry him and she had said yes. But as she was packing, the voices of her sisters, the wild Undines, kept taunting her through her window. They told her that you can't trust mortal men. They are always unfaithful. They are not made to be true. Undine, in her innocence, told them that Sir Hans would be different. And to prove them wrong, she made a pact with her sisters that if Sir Hans should prove unfaithful, she would kill him herself.

Love-drunk, the happy couple, having eyes for no one but each other, left on the bright sun-lit morning, after bidding the fisherman and his wife a heartfelt goodbye. They reached his castle and were married. They attend court where Undine meets Princess Bertha and where Sir Hans avoids Princess Bertha.

While at court, Undine, Princess Bertha and Sir Hans are thrown together much of the time. Bertha and Hans agree to let bygones be bygones, after all they do like each other (read: are still attracted to each other!). Bertha and Undine discover a sister-feeling in the fact that they were both raised by foster parents. The happy couple invite Bertha to come and live with them at their castle and she agrees.

Alas, as time goes on, Hans finds himself falling in love again with Bertha and she with him. Have I told you how strange Undine is? How she likes to be out in rain storms, how she speaks to snow flakes as if they are relatives? How she answers the trickles of fountains? I mean, what is a human male to do when he finds himself married to an elemental? Bertha, she is so nice, so predictable, so . . . human. And she knows how to cook and manage a castle.

Sir Hans begins to treat Undine poorly. He begins by withholding himself from her and not returning her love for him. Slowly he finds fault with the way she does things and upbraids her, while praising what Bertha does. Out of nowhere he erupts in anger. Soon he is yelling at her in front of the servants. Still in love with him, Undine tries hard to please him. She begs him to be patient with her and she warns him not to show anger towards her when they are anywhere near water.

Bertha and Hans are now meeting in secret. They say they are friends, but the electricity is building up between them. Even the maids and footmen are whispering about them.

Hearing that Bertha would

like a sail on the Danube, Undine proposes that the three of them go on a trip. During this outing, her all-knowing wild Undine sisters try to get Undine's attention, so they can warn her, but only succeed in scaring Bertha and the rest of the party. Unable to contain his anger, Sir Hans lashes out at Undine, verbally punishing her for the failure of the voyage. Undine, stricken to the core, weeping and moaning, tells him she now must leave him forever, pleads with him to remember his vows and be faithful, and then dives overboard into the great river. What began as a pleasure cruise returns as a funeral barge.

Sir Hans and Bertha do try to be faithful to the memory of Undine, but they can no longer hold their feelings in check for each other now that Undine is presumed dead. After a brief time of mourning, their nuptials are announced.

The night before the day of the wedding, Hans dreams of ravens, his family's traditional sign that death is near. He wakes up moody and apprehensive. The day is stormy, as if the water elementals were trying to prevent the marriage from taking place. The invited priest lives too far to make it and all the roads are flooded. Luckily another priest is found and the ceremony is performed in the castle as planned. As the newly-wed couple kiss, the stained glass window in the church is broken by a downpour of water, which drenches the bride and groom. They both go to their rooms to put on dry clothes.

While Hans is changing he hears a familiar tap at his door. The tap was Undine's style of knocking at his door before entering. When he opens the door, he finds Undine, who enters veiled and with bowed head. He is struck by her appearance and asks if she is an apparition. No, she says. He asks her if she is causing the storm and she tells him she was trying to give him one more chance to be faithful to her. He asks if he can see her face and she takes off her veil. Seeing her again, he is deeply struck by her loveliness and beauty. The ember of love sparks in his heart and then bursts into flame. They embrace. When they separate, Undine is weeping.

'Alas, you have given me no choice, I am here for your death,' she cries.

Feeling in his heart that this is right and so, he tells her that if he must die he would prefer to die in her embrace. Gently, lovingly and with great tenderness they kiss. As soon as her lips touch his, he dies.

At his funeral, right after the coffin is buried in the earth, the mourners notice the appearance of a tiny spring surrounding the grave of the dead knight.

We are now moving into the forbidden terrain of sexuality. Forbidden by the misogynist Church, that is. As women the key to recovering our sexuality lies in the wild feminine. As we learned in the Introduction, mermaids are the archetype of the wild feminine and our perfect guides.

Awakening your sexual self

Sexual energy is the dynamic energy that flows through creation. All animals, mammals, reptiles – in fact, anything and everything that reproduces, including the human being – are animated by sexual energy. It is one of the primal urges that comes with the package of incarnating in human form. Sexual energy is a restorative, deeply regenerative healing force, that isn't partner dependent for enjoyment. Sexual energy is the high-powered rocket fuel that explodes in a trail of artistic expression: writing, painting, dancing and music. Or it can be directed into creating children. It can also be used for empowerment or for spiritual knowledge.

Whether you choose to speak the language of sexual energy or not it is there in your life. If you've relegated sexual energy to the position of 'lost continent' in your life, this is the time to mount a full-fledged expedition to reclaim it in the name of the Feminine. With the mermaids to assist you, you will be in gentle, healing and safe hands. Let us now pause for a Mythological Moment to meet our next mermaid goddess guide, **La Sirene**.

Mythological Moment: La Sirene

Some say She is a separate goddess, a unique entity. Others say She is the sea aspect of Erzulie. La Sirene is a mermaid, one of the Haitian loa (spirits) and is many different things to many different people. Some say her favourite colours are white and gold. What is sometimes agreed upon is that La Sirene is vastly wealthy: all the riches of the sea are hers. She has been known to appear to those who call on her as a gorgeous, sensual and very sexy woman, undulating like the sea as she moves.

La Sirene has exquisite taste and likes the best of everything. She loves gold and jewels, things of beauty. Her offerings have occasionally included such luxury items as expensive perfume, champagne, caviar, lingerie and silk clothes. That being said, it is also true that she gives generously to her devotees. La Sirene likes to be courted and wooed. She is the sexual force personified, wild and untamed. She is the *grande diva* of *femme fatales*. She will help you with romance, and if She takes you under her wing, you'll have no shortage of sexual partners!

Now it's time for our tête-à-tête with Ms Glamorous Herself. You may even want to dress for the occasion!

Journey to La Sirene

Find a time and a place when and where you will not be disturbed. Sit, lie or stand with your spine straight and close your eyes. Surround yourself with white light by envisioning yourself inside a luminous egg. Now take a deep breath and release it with a sigh. Take another deep breath and release it with a moan. Take a last deep breath and release it with a snake-like hiss. Let your breathing return to normal.

See, sense or feel the entrance to a cave. It can be a cave that you know or one that exists in your imagination. Take a deep breath and as you exhale, stand at the mouth of the cave. Put your hand on the cave's opening. What does it feel like? Now enter the cave.

The cave is a good size, comfortably warm and well lit. You walk to the back of the cave and notice that it becomes a tunnel. You enter the tunnel and go down, down, down. Deeper and deeper and deeper. Down, down, down. Becoming more relaxed, letting go, going deeper. Down, down, down. Deeper and deeper and deeper. Until you reach the end where you see some different coloured light. On the count of three you will step out into the otherworld. One – two – three. Step out of the tunnel.

You are underwater, fully capable of breathing and completely at home. As you look down at your body, you see your legs transforming into a fish tail. You are now in your mermaid form. You see another mermaid swimming towards you. She is surrounded in a faint glow of golden light that her body gives off. It is La Sirene.

You greet her and she accepts your greeting. Then she takes your hand and tells you to come with her. You swim through the water until you come to the entrance of a cave, which you both enter. It is a large luxurious cave filled with the finest and most comfortable furniture. Crystal chandeliers provide the lighting, piles of gold and jewels glitter, and there is a huge open wardrobe filled with dazzling and provocative clothes. La Sirene tells you that she has an outfit that would look wonderful on you. She pulls it out from her wardrobe and hangs it up for you to see. From the moment you see the outfit, you know you will look marvellous in it.

La Sirene tells you just for fun she wants you to model it for her. You agree and suddenly you are wearing the outfit. The sensation you have wearing this clothing is beyond anything you've ever experienced with any clothing. You feel as if your skin has woken up and is now alive. You can feel your entire body in a different way. It is as if an electric current were running through you.

La Sirene takes you to her large mirror so you can see yourself. As you gaze at your reflection there is something different about you; a radiance, an allure, a being completely at ease within your body; perhaps even a sexuality that wasn't there before. You look totally present and vitally alive. While gazing into the mirror, you feel like walking around and you notice that you are moving differently. The centre of your gravity is low; it is in your hips and it feels good to let your hips flow freely. Your shoulders follow and you are standing up straight. Your chest is out and you feel wonderful.

'Now that's what you really look like, *ma chere*,' La Sirene comments, standing next to you in the mirror. She waves her hands over you and the outfit turns to a shimmering mist which is quickly absorbed into your body. As you continue to look in the mirror you notice that you still feel like the new you. It is time to return and you thank La Sirene. She gives you a dazzling smile and a wink and takes your hand. You leave the cave and swim back to the opening of the tunnel. La Sirene kisses you goodbye and swims off. You turn and as you enter the tunnel, you transform back to your original form, still feeling like the new you.

You are going up, up, up, feeling clear and clean, refreshed and revitalized, up, up, up, with a deepening sense of peace, lots of space and quiet within, up, up, up, awake and aware, till you re-enter the cave. You walk out of the mouth of the cave and take a deep breath. As you release it you are back in your body. You take another deep breath and as you release it you are more present in your body and can move it gently. You take a last deep breath and as you exhale you may open your eyes.

Welcome back! Don't forget to write down your thoughts in your journal.

Mermaid Tattoo

A 'too fabulous to be true' way to celebrate your newly recovered sexuality is to get a tattoo! There is something about body art that speaks primal, earthy, instinctual volumes. After all, 'nice' girls don't get tattoos!

A great way of keeping your Inner Mermaid in view is to wear her imprint somewhere on your body. Lucky for us modern mermaids, there are many ways to go about this. Here are two:

1. A temporary mermaid tattoo (see Resource Guide), or go on-line to find one. These last for a few days.
2. A henna tattoo (see Resource Guide), or go on-line to find one in your country.

I am partial to the henna choice. It lasts for about ten days or so and can be renewed. It is easy as there are places selling kits with instructions on how to mix your henna paste or you can purchase pre-mixed henna paste. What you will also need to either find or make yourself is a stencil.

To make a stencil, you will need some kind of sheet of plastic or rubbery type material. Henna needs to stay on the skin for roughly 30 minutes or more. Cardboard might or might not work as it can get soggy and you want a material that you can paste onto your skin and then apply the henna paste on to. A stiff but pliable piece of fabric, like oil cloth, might work.

Find a simple mermaid design that you like. Henna works best with a design with strong lines and shapes, not subtle shadings. A mermaid logo type of design would work well. You can draw one yourself to make the stencil or search on-line for one, print it out and then use it.

You may need the assistance of another pair of hands for your tattoo process. You might even want to give a henna tattooing party. Or you might have a Henna Parlour nearby or a local tattoo place that does henna body art. Whatever you choose to do about getting your henna tattoo, remember that you are gifting yourself in a *big way* by celebrating your recovered sexuality and honouring the beauty of your body! Expect powerful times ahead.

Now that you have recovered your sexuality, learned to adore and adorn yourself with mermaid baths and henna tattoos, and are frolicking in the sea of love, it is time to move on to the dance of romance.

Making magic for love

How do you know when is the right time to do magic for romance? Should you make magic to call in a lover or mate? What if you call in a lover or mate and find you aren't ready? These are just some of the questions you can ask your Inner Mermaid when you do the following journey. But before you do the meditation, write out what you would like to ask her in your journal. If you have written complex sentences, break them down into bite-sized pieces, so that you are very clear, direct and to the point. For example, you could ask questions such as:

✦ *Is it time for me to have a mate?*
✦ *Am I with the best partner for me?*
✦ *What do I need to do to call in a mate?*

By now you are on intimate terms with your Inner Mermaid. This would be an ideal time to ask her.

Journey to your Inner Mermaid for answers

Find a time and a place when and where you will not be disturbed. Play a tape or CD of ocean sounds, light a candle and place your journal beside you. Then sit, lie or stand comfortably with your spine straight and close your eyes. Surround yourself with white light by envisioning yourself inside a luminous egg. Take a long, slow, deep breath to the count of four (count to four while inhaling), then hold the breath for a count of four, and exhale to the count of four. Take another deep breath and this time breathe into your skin and as you exhale, breathe out of your skin. Take a deep breath and breathe into all the hairs on your body and as you exhale, breathe out of all the hairs on your body.

Focus on your heart chakra (which is located in the middle of your chest, near your heart) and breathe in and out of your heart chakra five times. Then focus on the quality of love and breathe love in and out of your heart chakra. Now, see, sense or feel the presence of your Inner Mermaid. When you feel her presence surrounding you,

you can begin to ask her your questions. You may want to write in your journal as you hear the answer or wait until the journey is over. It is up to you and your ability to be in two different realities at the same time.

When you have received what you need, thank your Inner Mermaid for spending time with you. She will ask you for a gift and you will give it with an open heart.

Breathe into your skin and as you exhale, breathe out of your skin. Breathe into all the hairs on your body and as you exhale, breathe out of all the hairs on your body. Now take a breath of electric energy that fizzles and crackles and as you exhale, send that electric energy throughout your body and open your eyes.

Welcome back!

If you've been given a clear message from your Inner Mermaid that the timing is good for you to go ahead and make magic for a mate, or lover, congratulations! You have reached the point where you are loving yourself, and therefore have love to give to others, and have done some working on self-healing and wholing.

If you haven't been given a clear answer to go ahead, I would suggest waiting until you are. You will be ready sometime soon. Patience, combined with the willingness to gain greater clarity on what needs healing from within, will reward you in due time with what you are desiring. And by holding off till a more appropriate time, you will have the inner resources to handle it when you do get what you want.

Asking for help from the mermaids

Your next step in making magic for a partner/lover/-mate/whatever involves a power meeting with **Ratu Rara Kidul**, the Queen, to ask for help in your love quest. Rara Kidul is a potent energy to be called upon and utmost respect is required. She is powerful and capricious, and if she chooses to help you, you will be blessed. However, she will need you to do something for her and you must do it with an open and willing heart. It will never be more than you can manage.

Let us pause for some mythological preparation before our appointment.

Mythological Moment: Ratu Rara Kidul

Known as the 'Queen of the South Seas' Ratu Rara Kidul is a Javanese mermaid goddess of Indonesia and a presence very much alive, acknowledged and respected in that culture. People to this day report sightings of Her Royal Highness emerging from her palace below the ocean and strolling on to the beach. Her favourite colour is green; no one can sport any garment of that colour while on the shore, for fear of insulting the Queen. Ratu Rara Kidul can be called on to assist in affairs of the heart and has a cycle of renewal that is connected to the cycles of the moon – a perfect mermaid for lunar magic.

Married to the fifteenth century historical sultan of Yogyakarta and Solo, Senopati, Rara Kidul is still treated, even today, as a venerated member of the family. In the pantheon of Javanese mythology, which originated in

India, Rara Kidul is sometimes associated with the Hindu goddess Kali's aspects of time, death and regeneration. Rara Kidul will appear as a beautiful young woman when the moon journeys from new to full and as a wise old woman when the moon goes from full to dark. She is worshiped by fishermen as an ocean goddess and by farmers as a rain and storm goddess, alike.

The night before the opening of the Samudra Beach Hotel in 1966 on the Javanese southern coast, Rara Kidul's territory, Sultan Buwono, member of the ruling house and one of Rara Kidul's descendants, was staying there as an invited guest. Much to his surprise, he was entreated for an audience by a local village headman. When granted, the man told him he had a dream in which a beautiful woman in green appeared and asked for her offerings. The sultan thanked the man, knowing full well he had seen Rara Kidul, and stated that he wouldn't be able to make the required offerings, because he was attending the opening in an official capacity, not in a spiritual or religious one. The headman, feeling a bit apprehensive, bowed to his sultan's wishes and left. Within the hour after the meeting, a huge tidal wave hit the hotel, drenching the guests and destroying the buffet table. The Sultan asked for a room for Rara Kidul and went and made the necessary offerings. The sea immediately became docile. To this day the Samudra Beach Hotel keeps that room vacant and in readiness for visits from the Queen.

Journey to Rara Kidul

Find a time and a place when and where you will not be disturbed. Sit, lie or stand with your spine straight and close your eyes. Surround yourself with white light by envisioning yourself inside a luminous egg. Take a deep breath and release it with a sigh. Take another deep breath and release it with a moan. Take a last deep breath and release it with a snake-like hiss. Let your breathing return to normal.

See, sense or feel the entrance to a cave. It can be a cave that you know or one that exists in your imagination. Take a deep breath and as you exhale, stand at the mouth of the cave. Put your hand on the cave's opening. What does it feel like? Now enter the cave.

The cave is a good size, comfortably warm and well lit. You walk to the back of the cave and notice that it becomes a tunnel. You enter the tunnel and go down, down, down. Deeper and deeper and deeper. Down, down, down. Becoming more relaxed, letting go, going deeper. Down, down, down. Deeper and deeper and deeper. Until you reach the end where you see some different coloured light. On the count of three you will step out into the otherworld. One – two – three. Step out of the tunnel.

You are standing on the threshold of Krang Tretes, the sacred cave of Ratu Rara Kidul and you have a large bouquet of rare orchids in your arms. You put the orchids down and immediately kneel down and touch your head to the ground. You hear someone approach and feel them touch you. It is Rara Kidul and she bids you rise. Dressed in shimmering green, as if the dress is made of millions of pieces of emerald, she welcomes you to her cave. You present her with the bouquet of orchids and she takes them graciously and smiles.

She beckons you over to an area with magnificent rich cushions in shades of green and a table where tea is set out. She first takes her seat, then gestures to you to take your seat too. She then claps her hands and the tea is served by invisible spirits. The taste of your tea is delicious and refreshing. Rara Kidul claps her hands again and this time music is played. The music is magically soothing and leaves you feeling rested and at peace. When the music is finished, Rara Kidul asks you what she can do for you. You tell her you would like her help in your quest for a mate or lover. She says she would be delighted to help. You ask her what she needs from you in order to do so. She tells you very clearly what she requires and you commit it to your memory. Then she stands up and you do so too. She thanks you for coming and paying her a visit. You give her a respectful bow, then turn and walk back to the entrance of this cave.

You step out of Krang Tretes and into the tunnel. Now

you are going up, up, up, feeling clear and clean, refreshed and revitalized; up, up, up, with a deepening sense of peace, lots of space and quiet within; up, up, up, awake and aware, till you re-enter the cave. You walk out of the mouth of the cave and take a deep breath. As you release it you are back in your body. You take another deep breath and as you release it you are more present in your body and can move it gently. You take a last deep breath and as you exhale you may open your eyes.

Welcome back!

Time to journal.

If Rara Kidul has given you something to do for her that requires time, by all means do it. When you have completed her request, then you will be ready for the following ritual for calling in a lover or mate. I would suggest that you make use of the Appendix on lunar magic at the back of this book, so that you can choose the most auspicious time for your ritual.

Ritual to call in a lover or mate

1. Find a time and a place when and where you will not be disturbed.

2. Light a green and pink candle.

3. Light some incense in your incense burner or use sound (chimes, drums, a bell, or chant an OM).

4. Surround yourself with white light by envisioning yourself inside a luminous egg.

5. See, sense or feel white light coming out of the palms of your hands and see, sense or feel yourself drawing a circle of light around you as you say the following, inwardly or out loud (or use your own words if you prefer): '*I intend the highest good.*'

6. While standing in the centre of the circle, breathe in and out of your heart chakra three times.

7. Now see, sense or feel love. When you have got a fix on the quality of love, breathe love in and out of your heart chakra three times.

8. Ask your Inner Mermaid to be present and feel her enter the circle. The energy quickens and rises.

9. Invite Rara Kidul to be present and feel her enter the circle. You feel the pulsing of more energy.

10. Ask the energy present to take the form of a ball. Put your hands out and feel the ball of energy between them. With you, your Inner Mermaid and Rara Kidul creating a triangle of energy within the circle, begin to chant inwardly or out loud your need: 'a mate' or 'a lover' or 'a husband' or 'a consort', or use your own words if you prefer. A single word chant is fine, as is a sentence. It is about what you feel comfortable with. Focus your thoughts on what you need, not the 'who'. If the 'who' isn't part of your path or your soul's plan, then focusing on them can only get in the way of your obtaining what you need.

11. See, sense or feel the ball of energy in your hand growing.

12. When it feels ready, mentally or physically hurl it out into the universe and stop your chanting.

13. Stand with total acceptance and openness and state inwardly or out loud: 'Welcome, he (or she) is here.'

Spend time chanting that until you feel the presence of who you have called to you as a reality.

14. Thank Rara Kidul for coming and release her with love and gratitude.

15. Thank your Inner Mermaid for coming and release her with love and gratitude.

16. Thank the white light for being present to create the circle, and release it with love and gratitude.

17. Blow out the candles.

18. Have a bite to eat to ground yourself. Mermaid tea (see page 28) and mermaid cakes (see page 172) would be especially good at this point!

19. Welcome back! Now write about your experience in your journal.

Now that you have done your romance ritual, you know your mate is here. Be sure to stay in the present with your thoughts about him/her. Universal Law states that we create our reality with our thoughts. If you think of your mate as 'coming' then that is what you will create and he/she won't be here now in the present. Remember to cultivate that attitude of gratitude and spend some time giving thanks for his/her presence in your life.

Becoming whole and complete again

Whenever we open to love, we bravely march onward, with little or no thoughts about potential wounds or risks to ourselves. It is when we become aware that things didn't work out as we had planned, that we take time to take stock of our hurting places. Casualties accrue from giving too big a piece of ourselves to the other, leaving gaping holes in ourselves and our lives. What we need to speed up the healing process is to become a virgin – and by virgin I mean whole and complete unto herself – again.

Britomartis is the perfect mermaid goddess to guide you into the wholeness of your feminine power. You'll be meeting her several times within these pages.

Mythological Moment: Britomartis

Britomartis, one of the most powerful goddesses of the high civilization of Minoan Crete, was a very ancient goddess. Some say that when the younger civilization of Hellenic Greece[13] invaded the far older culture of Crete, the attributes of the goddess Britomartis were grafted on to Artemis[14], for whom she was a prototype. Worshipped in difficult to reach mountain temples, Britomartis is a maiden goddess of the hunt, known to have gifted humans with the use of fishing nets. She is also a goddess associated with wild mountain places, animals, transformation, regeneration and birth. Her animal is the snake.

Her story is that she was a young sweet virgin, a mortal woman, who was pursued by King Minos through the forests, across the mountains, over streams and rivers, across rocky landscapes. Try as he might, Minos tried to catch Britomartis and for nine long months she succeeded in eluding his grasp. Finally, she was run to ground on a steep cliff overlooking the ocean. Rather than give in to

him, she threw herself into the frothy sea. She was saved
by some fishnets and transformed into an immortal.

The following special mermaid magic ritual is ideal for
creating wholeness when you have given away too much
of yourself to your former love.

You may want to check in the Appendix on lunar
magic to choose the time when the energies of the moon
will work with you. Since this is a healing ritual you can
do it when the moon is in Virgo for healing, or when the
moon is in Aries for selfhood, or Scorpio for healing the
passions. The best advice, however, is to do it when it feels
right to you!

Re-virgining ritual

1. Light a white candle.

2. Surround yourself with white light.

3. Breathe love in and out from your heart chakra.

4. Focus on your Inner Mermaid and ask her to be present at this ritual.

5. Invite Britomartis to be present.

6. Form a triangle of energy by sending out a strand of energy from your heart to the heart of your Inner Mermaid, and then from her heart to the heart of Britomartis and back to you.

7. Focus on the pulsing of that triangle of energy connecting your heart and the two mermaids.

8. Ask that the piece or pieces that you gave _____ (name him or her) come back to you now. For example, your playful piece, your ability to love piece, your personal independence which you might have traded for some dependence or interdependence, and so on. Britomartis names the piece or pieces as they appear inside the triangle, until all your pieces are there.

9. You say the name of each piece out loud and take a moment to take it in. Do this until all the pieces are absorbed.

10. Notice that you feel stronger, more energetic, filled with vitality.

11. Take the strand of energy connecting the three hearts back into your heart.

12. Bid farewell to Britomartis and release her with gratitude.

13. Thank your Inner Mermaid and release her with gratitude.

14. Thank yourself and give yourself an inner hug.

15. Blow out the candle.

16. Give yourself some silent time to journal your experience.

Gaining perspective

Taking your love to the next step has to do with your willingness to work on what comes up for you in your relationship. You can do magic to call in a mate or lover, but then the magic you do to create the right relationship is about how much you are willing to see and heal yourself when your buttons are being pushed. What helps when your emotions are closing in on you and blinding you to anything but their view of reality is to gain perspective.

Atargatis has consented to be of service in helping us gain a more balanced view of our reality. Let us pause and find out more about her, before we journey to her.

Mythological Moment: Atargatis

Atargatis, the mermaid great mother goddess of Syria, was called upon to provide abundant crops, for she was the very essence of moisture that the plants depended on for their life and fertility. She also ruled the sky, appearing arrayed in clouds with eagles for a headdress. When danger threatened the security of her Syrian cities, Atargatis was appealed to to ensure their impregnable defences. She was said to have kept a pond of oracular fish, and that a great magical dove laid the egg out of which she was hatched. Out of respect for her, the Syrians did not consume either fish or doves.

Her daughter, the goddess Semiramis, was born of her union with a beautiful mortal boy. To ensure that he would be hers, and hers only, she caused him to vanish. After making sure her daughter would be attended to by doves, Atargatis retreated to a lake and there transformed into the Great Fish Mother. Some say her husband was the god Haddad. Others say that she is a combination of two other great goddesses: Anat and Astarte.

Atargatis can be invoked for assistance with issues of security, abundance, fertility and relationships. She says that if you develop a strong connection with her, she would be willing to aid you with even more!

Journey to Atargatis

Find a time and a place when and where you will not be disturbed. Sit, lie or stand with your spine straight and close your eyes. Surround yourself with white light by envisioning yourself inside a luminous egg. Take a deep breath and release it with a sigh. Take another deep breath and release it with a moan. Take a last deep breath and release it with a snake-like hiss. Let your breathing return to normal.

See, sense or feel an enormous tree. A tree so big that you practically have to lie down to see how high the branches extend. It can be one that you know or one that exists in your imagination. Now stand next to the tree. Run your hand over the bark of the tree. How does it feel? Walk around the tree till you find an entrance. Now enter the tree.

Inside the tree there is a wonderful woodsy smell and lots of space. There are two signs that lead in different directions: one says UP and the other, DOWN. You follow the sign going UP. Now you are travelling in a large branch that is ascending. The branch is spacious, warm and well lit. You are travelling up, up, up. Letting go and giving over to the sensation of floating. Up, up, up. Feeling more and more relaxed. Up, up, up. Feeling safe and secure, until you come to the end of the large branch.

You hear a screech and see a very large eagle before you. The eagle is there to take you to Atargatis. You climb on the eagle and the eagle flies off, soaring through the air, riding on the wind, till it begins its descent and lands on the ground by a lake. You dismount and the eagle flies off.

You see the lone figure of a woman, feeding a flock of doves, and you go over to her. It is Atargatis and she welcomes you with a warm and loving hug. She asks you why you are here and you tell her that you need her help in gaining perspective over your emotions. She agrees to help you.

She takes your hand and leads you over to a rocky promontory where two chairs and a table are set up. You are seated and notice that if you look right down you can see into the lake. The water is very clear. Atargatis sits in the chair next to you. She explains to you that this is a magical lake that she uses to gain clarity in her life. All that she has to do is focus on what she is needing perspective on and put her hand in the lake and the lake will reflect what she needs to see, sense or feel.

Atargatis asks you to take a deep breath and as you exhale to bring to mind what you are needing clarity on. You do so. She then tells you that when you are ready, to put your hand in the lake. You reach down and place your hand in the lake. Suddenly the waters take on a life of their own. They swirl and froth, bubble and stir until they settle down into a film-like series of images for you. They are images from your life. You find you are able to watch them without emotion or feeling. You watch them as an observer. There is detachment in the viewing and you are able to achieve exactly what you need.

Seeing what you need enables you to gain clarity on what action you need to take. This brings you a great sense of comfort and ease, a feeling of joy and freedom. When you have seen all that you need, you take your hand out of the water. You turn to Atargatis, who is smiling at you, and you thank her. She thanks you for being willing to see. Then she asks you for a gift and you give it to her with an open heart.

It is now time to return. A very big eagle comes in for a landing. You mount the eagle and it takes off and soars through the sky. It deposits you on a sturdy branch with a large opening.

You enter the branch of your enormous tree. Now you are going down, down, down, feeling energized and full; down, down, down, feeling changed and different; down, down, down, feeling strong and sure. You have now arrived in the trunk of the tree. You can see light at the opening of the tree. You walk out into the light. You are standing next to the tree.

Take a deep breath and as you exhale, feel yourself coming back into your body. Take another deep breath and as you exhale, move your body gently. Take a final deep breath and when you are ready, open your eyes.

Welcome back!

Give yourself some extra time to journal to ensure that this journey is taken in deep.

Calling it quits

One of the greatest challenges on the playing field of love is ending a relationship that no longer works, no matter how hard you both have tried. You know it is time to end it because you are causing each other pain, *but* you both still love each other ... What do you do?

You contact the great mermaid goddess **Yemanja** for some emergency heart repair aid, and ask her to help you in calling it quits.

Ritual for ending a painful affair

In the following ritual we are going to work with the concept of offerings. Offerings are special acts of service. Making an offering is an expenditure of energy. One reason why they are good for this particular ritual is that they use your wounded, hurt and grieving energy in their making and transform that energy into something beautiful and loving that will help heal your heart.

Offerings come in many shapes, sizes and styles. Therefore, making an offering is very, very simple. If you are comfortable with cooking, you can bake a cake; if you feel at home arranging flowers, make a flower arrangement; if the sensuous world of scents is where you swim best, then make an organic cologne using essential oils. You might want to check in with Yemanja to ask what she would like from you for an offering. If so, do the **Journey to Yemanja** (see page 64) and ask.

PREPARATION

1. Make/prepare your offering according to what Yemanja would like.

2. Include in the offering a symbol of your ex-love. It could be something that has his/her energy on it, or a picture, or something that you make or buy that is him/her.

3. If Yemanja hasn't specified a time to do the ritual, see the Appendix on lunar magic at the back of the book to choose the best time that will work for you. My suggestion is when the moon is decreasing – going to the dark of the moon.

4. If you have special ritual clothes, such as a shawl, scarves, a silk outfit, poncho, anything that you don't wear for everyday activities but keep for magical occasions, plan to wear them for the ritual.

5. You may want to do this either solo or with a bevy of mermaid sisters.

6. If you are living near an ocean or can plan a trip to the ocean for this ritual, then do so. If not, then find a large body of water near you and use that.

7. Pack what you will need for your ritual: blue and white candles; incense and incense burner; matches; flowers in a vase or basket, and anything else you think would be good for a temporary altar. You might want to bring along some objects from your altar at home, plus some food that Yemanja would like, such as watermelon or any other type of melon. Put on your ritual clothes or take them with you to put on when you get there.

8. Choose a time when you can have access to the body of water without attracting too much attention.

PERFORMING YOUR RITUAL

1. When you arrive at the beach (or your chosen place for the ritual), make a rough altar for Yemanja, placing the offering for her in the centre.

2. Light the candles.

3. Light the incense.

4. Invoke Yemanja and tell her you are here. Explain why you need her help and what you want to achieve – freedom from the love that is causing you pain.

5. If you are with mermaid sisters, you might like to chant or sing together for Yemanja. If you are alone, then you might choose to chant or sing silently, or out loud. You can use a chant or song that you know, or one that you make up yourself. The simplest chant uses one word 'Yemanja', and all you do is chant it over and over again.

6. When the energy feels right, pick up the offering and go to the water.

7. If you feel comfortable going into the water, do so, and carry the offering into the water. If not, set the offering in the water.

8. Watch what happens with your offering. Does the water take it or is it returned to you?

9. If the water takes it then thank Yemanja.

10. If the water doesn't take it, thank Yemanja.

11. Return to the altar and thank Yemanja for coming and release her with love and gratitude.

12. Blow out the candles.

13. Pack up all you have brought with you.

14. When you return home, write up your experience of

this ritual and keep close to your journal for the next week or so. Be sure to keep track of any changes.

15. If the water doesn't take your offering, do the **Journey to Yemanja** on page 64 to find out why she didn't accept your offering as there could be many, many reasons why, and ask Yemanja for advice on what to do, then follow it.

A final magical ritual for love

For land-born mermaids who want to take their romance into the deeper waters, here is a simple ritual that can help things open up magically.

Appreciation ritual

This ritual is to be done by both parties before bed.

1. Breathe in and out of your heart chakras.
2. Give your partner three appreciations. It can be about something that they have done, for example, appreciation for support, for cooking you breakfast, for taking the dog for a run, for giving you extra loving when you had your period. It is even better, however, if they are things that you notice about your partner and want to give voice to, such as their infectious laugh, a unique thing they do when they make love, the sound of their voice, their inner strength, how reliable they are, and so on.
3. Take in to your heart three appreciations that your partner gives you in return.

With our wellsprings full up and charged with love, with our lives now over-flowing with love for our unique selves, whether we consciously choosing to swim solo or paired, we are now ready to begin building on what we have. In our next steps as new-born/fledgling Mermaid Magicians we will learn to weave the mantles of protection and personal power, using, of course, those glistening strands of love.

CHAPTER 4

Mermaid Magic for Protection & Personal Power

Welcome to protection and personal power, mermaid style. No fainting, fragile females are they. All the power and protection, that was part and parcel of the make up of the feminine in matrilineal civilizations, and was trashed and forbidden by the Church, resides in profusion in these formidable fish-tailed *femmes*. If you are waffling about taking back your power, or are fearful about setting good boundaries, read no further. Warning: strong, creative play zone ahead!

Protecting yourself with mermaid magic

Is protection today different from what it was to our ancestors? Our ancestors called upon the good graces of their goddesses and gods just to stay alive. Theirs was a world filled with countless daily threats to their continued existence. As we learned in Chapter 1, the Greeks called upon the mermaids affiliated with protection prior to undertaking any sailing venture. Although the challenges are now different in our twenty-first century lives, we still find ourselves in need of regular safe-keeping from any potential harm. Hence our creation of that billion dollar commercial enterprise: the insurance industry.

The best insurance policy, I believe, however, is the one we create ourselves with the assistance of the mermaids. I would rephrase one old adage: 'Trust in Allah, but tie up your camel,' to read: 'Make magic with the mermaids, but renew your auto, boat, homeowner, health and life insurance.' In other words, take care of the physical plane with good common-sense and work with the mermaids on the inner planes to make your everyday physical plane activities more powerful and fun!

As we have already experienced in the journeys and rituals in this book, one of the quickest ways of creating protection is by surrounding ourselves with white light. Now we are about to discover another fabulous way of protecting ourselves – this time involving our Inner Mermaid and her magic. With Her help, we are going to discover the protective power of the seashell in the following journey and ritual.

Seashells have been protecting and housing marine life forever. Their beautiful shape, graceful form and strong resilient material has made collectors out of any one and everyone. Aphrodite, Great Goddess and mermaid archetype, was said by the Greeks to have been born of the sea. She rose out of the waves and floated to shore on Her very own protective covering: a sea shell. What better protection for us on our path through life than that which served the great Goddess, Aphrodite.

Seashell shield journey

Find a time and a place when and where you will not be disturbed. If you have a cassette tape or CD of ocean sounds, put it on. Sit, stand or lie comfortably with your spine straight and close your eyes. Surround yourself with white light by envisioning yourself inside a luminous egg.

Breathe in relaxation and peace and let it fill your body. Breathe out a sigh of relief. Breathe in calm, focused clarity and breathe out any tension. When you are ready, breathe love in and out of your heart chakra and establish contact with your Inner Mermaid by seeing, feeling or sensing her presence. You feel her presence sparkling in the air around you. You both exchange love and she asks you what you need. You tell her you need her help with creating protection.

She tells you she has just the perfect thing for you. She tells you to take a breath of love in and out through your heart chakra, with the conscious intent to build up your stores of love. Now she tells you to move the love up from your heart chakra to your third eye and you do so. As you hold love in your third eye, she tells you to use the love, now combined with light or wisdom in the third eye, to weave a seashell shield around you.

You ask her to help you with this and you feel a stronger presence directing the movement of the love-light from your third eye. Now you begin to feel as if you are standing in a seashell that is being woven from love-light coming out of your third eye. Your Inner Mermaid tells you to continue to breathe love in and out, because your seashell shield needs more love, and you do so.

As the shield is completed, you experience a deep sense of safety, security and protection. You revel as you swim about in a shield made of love. You thank your Inner Mermaid and she asks you for a gift. You give it to her with an open heart.

Now you are ready to return. Focus on your heart chakra. Breathe in and out of your heart chakra, three times. Take a deep breath and as you exhale open your eyes.

Welcome back!

Time to journal your experience.

Ritual for activating your seashell shield

Now that you have created your seashell shield, it is time to activate it and bring it into daily use and awareness. A really helpful way to do this is to use a tangible, real seashell, as a reminder.

You may have a seashell in your collection of things. If you do, first ask the shell if it would like to be used as part of this ritual. If it agrees, then proceed. If it doesn't, and if you don't happen to have a seashell on hand, you will need to either go to the sea and get one or go on-line (or to a local shop) to purchase one. You will also need a bowl of sea water or salt water that you make yourself. I would suggest that you do this ritual anytime on or before the full moon because you want to increase your protection. Lastly, prior to this ritual, place your seashell and the bowl of water on your altar.

I am using the term 'touch object' instead of touchstone in the following ritual – and this is something that you can touch to evoke something else. In this case you will touch your seashell and your seashell shield will be activated.

Now you are ready to do the ritual:

1. Find a time and a place when and where you will not be disturbed.
2. Light a white candle.
3. Surround yourself with white light by envisioning yourself inside a luminous egg.
4. Place your seashell in the bowl of water on your altar.
5. Invoke your favourite mermaid goddess for assistance.
6. Ask your Inner Mermaid to be present.
7. Create a triangle of energy by sending out love from your heart chakra to the mermaid goddess, then to your Inner Mermaid, and then back to you.
8. In your own words, or the following words, ask that this seashell be consecrated for use by you as a touch object for protection. '*I call on the power and presence and willingness of this seashell to be used as a touch object by me for protection.*'
9. Take the seashell out of the water.
10. In your own words, or the following words, ask that

this seashell be the physical representation of your seashell shield. And that when you touch it with the intent that your shield be activated to protect you, it shall. '*I ask that this seashell be the physical representation of my seashell shield and that when I touch it with the intent that my shield be activated to protect me, it shall.*'

11. Wait until you feel what you have just asked for happen.

12. Thank the mermaid goddess and release her with gratitude.

13. Thank your Inner Mermaid and release her with gratitude.

14. Thank the seashell and put it back on your altar, or in your pocket, or hang it on a chain around your neck.

15. Blow out your candle.

Above everything else, the best protection from potential harm is a loving heart. One that is filled with gratitude for all that comes its way. And as we have discovered, the best insurance is the seashell shield. Another way to protect your body from absorbing negativity is to wear silk clothes. And if you find yourself in the middle of a life over-flowing with negativity, almost as if you are a magnet, quick, do the journey to your Inner Mermaid and ask for help.

Now that we have our protection firmly in place and our seashells at the ready, we have created a solid port from which to set sail on a smashing voyage of self-empowerment. Some of the ways we will be discovering and building our power will be taking us to Crete, the Baltic Sea and England, and involve such diverse activities as making our own amber and coral beads and baking cakes. So hang on for an eclectic and power-fuelled joyous ride!

Recovering your feminine power

Personal power does not mean 'power over femininity', but rather you stepping into your own power and becoming empowered. Where are the areas in your life that you lack power? What would being a powerful person feel like to you? Do you fear power? Are you a high-powered female executive who exudes power in the way of being the 'best man for the job'? If so, then you may want to delve into and recover your feminine power.

Why is it important to recover feminine power? Because we are strangers in a strange culture: we live in a masculine world with masculine values. The feminine has long been invalidated. To restore the balance between the male and female we need to recover our feminine power.

The Mermaid Interlude in this chapter on page 163 was chosen with that in mind. Since the mermaids are archetypes of the wild feminine, and the wild feminine includes freedom, being whole and complete unto yourself, sexuality and power, the more we spend time with them the more we will absorb their feminine ways.

Naming is also an important way to gain power. This is one of the reasons why language is so important. (We only need to look at how everything in our society is referred to with the pronoun 'he', whether it means a man or not.) In the old days names were thought to contain the very essence of power. Warriors would recite their personal and family names before battle. It assisted them in calling on the power in both their names and those of their ancestors. In other cultures, you would never use a person's real name (it was a secret name known only to them), because it was believed to hold too much power. You would use a nickname instead. Even today, look at what happens when you are able to affix a name to a formless fear. It no longer has power over you.

In the following journey the mermaid goddess Britomartis will help us to name the parts of our life where we feel disempowered, so we can then take steps to empower ourselves in these areas. Britomartis is an ancient Cretian mermaid goddess, whom we met in the last chapter. She is the perfect archetype for the virgin – one who is whole and complete unto herself – and therefore, just right to assist us in our empowerment journey.

In the journey, Britomartis will scan our body, stopping over the places where we might feel disempowered or wounded. This is because disempowerment shows up in different parts of our body. So if we are disempowered in our love relationships, for example, it will show up in our heart. If we have been wounded sexually, it will show up in our genitals and womb. And if we feel disempowered as women, it could also show up in our womb, breasts and hips.

Journey to Britomartis

Find a time and a place when and where you will not be disturbed. Sit, lie or stand with your spine straight and close your eyes. Surround yourself with white light by envisioning yourself inside a luminous egg. Take a deep breath and release it with a sigh. Take another deep breath and release it with a moan. Take a last deep breath and release it with a snake-like hiss. Let your breathing return to normal.

See, sense or feel the entrance to a cave. It can be a cave that you know or one that exists in your imagination. Take a deep breath and as you exhale, stand at the mouth of the cave. Put your hand on the cave's opening. What does it feel like? Now enter the cave.

The cave is a good size, comfortably warm and well lit. You walk to the back of the cave and notice that it becomes a tunnel. You enter the tunnel and go down, down, down. Deeper and deeper and deeper. Down, down, down. Becoming more relaxed, letting go, going deeper. Down, down, down. Deeper and deeper and deeper. Until you reach the end where you see some different coloured light. On the count of three you will step out into the otherworld. One – two – three. Step out of the tunnel.

You are standing in brilliant sunlight on a rocky path. A very tall, statuesque young woman equipped with a bow and quiver of arrows comes to greet you. It is Britomartis. She is delighted to see you. She takes your hand and tells you it is a short walk to the lagoon. When you reach the lagoon Britomartis invites you to sit down on a chaise longue and she sits next to you. She asks you the purpose of your visit. You tell her that you would like to recover your feminine power and you need her help with naming the areas of your life where you feel disempowered. She smiles and nods her head. She understands and tells you she will help.

Britomartis stands up and tells you to lie down. She kneels in the sand beside you and holds her hands, palms down, over your body. She begins by running her hands one foot above your body, as if scanning. She is searching for what is interfering with you being in your power. Her hands stop over the place or places on your body which correspond to where you are disempowered or wounded in regards to your power. She then removes the object that has caused the wound and you immediately feel better. You feel your energy and power flowing. You feel stronger and more vital. Britomartis puts healing energy into the wound and restores it. She then whispers a word or some words in your ear that are meant for you alone, to be used daily as a mantra to facilitate the healing of your power.

She helps you to sit up again and you both gaze deep into each other's eyes. She then tells you the area or areas in which you are disempowered, and that you are a beautiful vessel of feminine power. You thank her and she asks you for a gift. You give her the gift with an open heart.

It is time to return. You both get to your feet and then Britomartis takes your hand and leads you back onto the path. You easily find the opening of the tunnel and you enter.

Now you are going up, up, up, feeling clear and clean, refreshed and revitalized, up, up, up, with a deepening sense of peace, lots of space and quiet within, up, up, up, awake and aware, till you re-enter the cave. You walk out of the mouth of the cave and take a deep breath. As you release it you are back in your body. You take another deep breath and as you release it you are more present in your body and can move it gently. You take a last deep breath and as you exhale you may open your eyes.

Welcome back!

Remember to record this and all your journey and ritual experiences in your journal. Writing, which is a left-brained task, after doing something with your right brain, helps to synchronize your brain hemispheres. It also reinforces the healing and wholing you experienced.

Don't worry if there are things that you can't quite remember. They are there and will come back to you when you are ready to know and make use of them. When you write about your area or areas of disempowerment, you want to phrase it in the positive, because energy follows thought and you want to stop the disempowerment, not continue it. For example, if you feel a lack of power when you speak, then you would want to empower yourself with easy, clear and effective communication. If your sexual power was dampened down or destroyed, you would want to reinstate it with joyful, loving acceptance.

Mermaid power necklace

This is another one of those ambitious little projects that serve a multitude of magical purposes. The mermaid power necklace is a tool for empowerment that consists of beads which you make and, if so desired, other significant mermaidy objects. Each of the beads will highlight an area of your life where you have formerly felt disempowered – but now, thanks to your Journey to Britomartis, you are healing nicely – and are willing to take your power back. For example, if you were disempowered in your ability to speak your truth, then you might want to make a bead that is about speaking without fear. If you were squashed sexually and don't relish your womanliness, you might want to make a bead that celebrates your body or just your womb!

There are so many ways you can make this necklace. It is great to do alone or with a bunch of mermaid friends. You can choose to make one bead at a time, or make the entire necklace in one day. You can entice your creativity by choosing to make all the beads needed, or you can make one fabulous bead and purchase the rest. You can use part beads, part seashells, or part whatever captures your imagination. This is the time to let your raw creativity go wild. The mermaid power necklace lends itself to many variations.

The medium we will be working in is polymer clay. It comes in many brands. Premo is the one I am experienced with and have listed here. If you choose another brand, you may have to adjust the amounts. Be sure to pick a brand that is used to make jewellery. Not all of them are. Polymer clay is a very affordable and safe medium. When you bake the clay, you will want to use a tent of aluminum foil to protect your oven or toaster oven, and you will want to be sure not to breathe in the fumes, but to ventilate your kitchen. One artist suggested using a separate toast oven outside. If you do plan to get very involved with this art form, this is an excellent idea.

Used in this necklace are faux amber and coral beads. Since coral is an endangered species, making your own coral is the most environmentally correct thing to do.

The following is a list of ingredients and tools you will need. You can purchase them locally at an arts supply store or on-line.

INGREDIENTS AND TOOLS

✦ *Premo brand of polymer clay:*
  2 packets red
  1 packet zinc yellow
  1 packet alizaran crimson
  2 packets golden yellow
  1 packet translucent

✦ *a work surface of wood or ceramic tile or formica or glass*
✦ *a modelling knife*
✦ *a glass roller*
✦ *a knitting needle for the holes in the beads*
✦ *a piece of clean cardboard*
✦ *wet or dry sandpaper, grit 400, 600 and 800 (very fine grades recommended for fine finishing and polishing)*
✦ *varnish – if you would like to varnish your beads, then ask your supplier which varnish is the best for this project.*

After you have purchased the supplies, you are ready to make beads! You may want to read your journal entry for the journey you did with Britomartis on page 138, or you may want to do the journey again.

Making faux amber beads

WHAT YOU WILL NEED ...

✦ *Polymer clay:*
  1 packet translucent
  ½ packet zinc yellow
  ¹⁄₁₆ packet alizaran crimson

INSTRUCTIONS

1. To make the amber, you condition the translucent clay by working it in the palms of your hands. It becomes soft or conditioned from the heat in your hands. Once you have done this, roll it out on the work area into a long log and then fold it in half and roll it out again. Keep doing this until the clay becomes pliable.

2. Condition the zinc yellow and alizaran crimson clay as above.

3. Add them to the translucent clay. Keep rolling the clay on the workspace with your palms and then fold in half and roll out again. Leave some streaks in the clay. This will give you an orange amber.

4. Divide the orange amber in half and put one piece aside.

5. Take half of the orange amber and add some yellow zinc and translucent. Make as before.

6. Now you have two colours of amber. Form your beads. If you need some ideas, do an on-line search for amber beads.

7. Be sure to remember to put holes in your beads before baking them (see instructions on page 149 for baking).

Making faux coral beads

WHAT YOU WILL NEED ...

✦ *Polymer clay:*

Batch 1:
1 packet red
½ packet golden yellow
¼ packet alizaran crimson

Batch 2:
¼ packet red
1 packet golden yellow

Batch 3:
½ packet red
½ packet golden yellow

Coral comes in a variety of colours and the above will give
you three different shades.

INSTRUCTIONS

1. To make the coral, combine the first batch and work as you did for the amber (see page 146). Set aside.
2. Form the second batch and work as above. Set aside.
3. Form the third batch and work as above. Set aside.
4. When your coral is ready, form into beads and put holes in the beads. Now they are ready for baking.

FINISHING YOUR BEADS

1. To bake, set your oven on 135°C/275°F and preheat.
2. You can put your beads on a wooden skewer. If your beads are round this is a good way to bake them. If you have large beads that are flattish, then place them on the clean cardboard.
3. You will need to bake your beads for 15 minutes for every $1/2$ cm/$1/4$ inch of thickness. Do not over-bake or burn your beads.
4. After the beads are baked, let them cool.
5. After the beads are cooled, it is time to sand them. You will want to sand them at your sink with running water. This ensures that the dust from sanding

won't get into your lungs. Begin with the lowest grade of sandpaper and move upwards.

6. When your beads are sanded, it is time to buff them.

7. After buffing you may want to varnish them.

8. When your beads are finished, you will want to charge them with mermaid empowerment (see ritual below). Once charged, place your beads on your altar, either separately or already arranged and designed in your necklace.

Now it is time to tear yourself away from those dazzling and exquisite beads – while extracting a promise to yourself to spend more time in Polymer-clay land – and move proudly on to our next ritual.

Ritual to consecrate and name your beads

Since you are wanting your power to grow and heal, a good time to do this ritual is when the moon is heading towards fullness. You might want to check with the Appendix on lunar magic at the back of the book so you can choose the most auspicious time for your ritual.

When you are ready:

1. Light a candle.
2. Surround yourself with white light by envisioning yourself inside a luminous egg.
3. Breathe love in and out of your heart chakra.
4. Focus on your Inner Mermaid and establish contact by seeing, feeling or sensing her presence.
5. Ask if she will flow the empowering energy of the mermaids through you. When she agrees, continue.
6. Pick up your first (or first and only) bead and hold it to your heart.
7. Feel the empowering mermaid energy build up in your heart.

8. When there is a strong build up of energy, will the empowering mermaid energy into the bead and state out loud what the bead is for. For example: '*I charge this bead with communication and take my power back in communication.*'

9. Feel, sense or see the bead you are holding become charged with the energy you have invoked.

10. When the bead feels done, replace it and go on to the next one, and so on until all the beads are finished.

11. Take a deep breath and as you exhale stop the flow of energy.

12. Give thanks to your Inner Mermaid.

13. Focus on breathing love in and out of your heart chakra.

14. Blow out the candle.

15. If you feel a strong build up of energy in your body, you can place your hands on the ground and give it back to the earth.

16. Write about this experience in your journal.

This is a good time for some mermaid tea (see page 281) and mermaid cakes (see page 172) to ground yourself after the ritual. If your necklace is finished, then put it on saying these words or their equivalent:

> *'My personal power is flowing through me*
> *in all areas in my life.'*

Take a slow deep breath as you feel the life force hum through the necklace prior to putting it on.

If your necklace needs to be completed, then complete it when you feel is the right time. Remember to use the above statement and to feel the necklace come to life prior to putting it on.

Creating the best for ourselves

We all want to create the best possible life for ourselves; however, ironic though it may seem, none of us have received any training in how to do that. Here is where the mermaids can be of special help.

There may be something in your life which you don't feel good about. Find out what it is, then choose to create a better situation. If it is something that absolutely cannot be changed, then choose to create an inner shift. Accept that it is in your life, and change your attitude to it. We may not be able to control what happens to us. But we can control how we choose to be with whatever happens. And we can choose to create the very best for ourselves, our loved ones and our world, no matter what happens.

Let's pause now for a Mythological Moment and meet our next mermaid goddess, **Jurate**, who can help us navigate the obstacles in our lives, support us when we heed the call of humanitarian pursuits and rally us to take back our sovereignty.

Mythological Moment: Jurate

In the time of the Old Ones, and in the deeps of the Baltic Sea, lived the radiant and independent mermaid Jurate, Goddess of the Sea. She lived in a palace made of amber, with amber furniture, amber plates, even amber forks and knives. She was free and independent and could do what she liked. She ruled wisely over the mer-folk and if asked with respect, would always allow her waters to be fished.

One day she noticed Kastytis - a new fisherman who hadn't asked, made the usual offerings or acknowledged her jurisdiction over the sea - boldly throwing his nets in and taking whatever fish he pleased. This angered Jurate so she dispatched a whole school of her mermaids to evict this mortal from her territory. Watching from nearby, she saw how the fisherman didn't bat an eye at her troops, although they batted many an eye at him. He just kept right on throwing in his nets and hauling out her fish.

Deciding to make short work of him herself, she swam close to his boat, positioning herself so he would have to see her. When he looked at her and she at him, love struck them both simultaneously. Kastytis, right then and there, left his life on land and joined Jurate beneath the sea in her amber palace.

After spending a few blissful days together, they got married, swearing to love and cherish the love they shared in this lifetime and beyond.

Unbeknownst to Jurate, her possessive father, Perkunas, God of Thunder, deciding to impose his will upon her freedom and sovereignty, had promised her to Patrimpas, God of Water. When he discovered that his immortal daughter had wed a mortal man, he acted swiftly and with great ferocity. An enormous mega-ton fire bolt descended from sky to sea and exploded the amber palace of Jurate.

When the sea returned to calm, and the rubble from the palace cleared, nothing was left of Kastytis. Jurate went wild with grief. However, not content with the destruction of his daughter's love, Perkunas devised a wicked punishment and chained Jurate to the wreckage of her former home and place of happiness. There she continues to this very day, grieving her loss and providing food for those who fish in her waters. When Lithuanians find amber in small perfect tear-drop pieces, they say these are the tears of Jurate.

And now we are ready to journey to meet our Lithuanian mermaid of the Baltic Sea, Jurate.

Journey to Jurate

Find a time and a place when and where you will not be disturbed. Sit, lie or stand with your spine straight and close your eyes. Surround yourself with white light by envisioning yourself inside a luminous egg. Take a deep breath and release it with a sigh. Take another deep breath and release it with a moan. Take a last deep breath and release it with a snake-like hiss. Let your breathing return to normal.

See, sense or feel the entrance to a cave. It can be a cave that you know or one that exists in your imagination. Take a deep breath and as you exhale, stand at the mouth of the cave. Put your hand on the cave's opening. What does it feel like? Now enter the cave.

The cave is a good size, comfortably warm and well-lit. You walk to the back of the cave and notice that it becomes a tunnel. You enter the tunnel and go down, down, down. Deeper and deeper and deeper. Down, down, down. Becoming more relaxed, letting go, going deeper. Down, down, down. Deeper and deeper and deeper. Until you reach the end where you see some different coloured light. On the count of three you will step out into the otherworld. One – two – three. Step out of the tunnel.

You are underneath the Baltic Sea at the ruins of Jurate's amber palace. There are chunks of amber in all shapes and sizes and you wander among them. You come to a pile of tiny amber tears, which leads you to where Jurate is chained.

The chains that bind Jurate are strong and heavy. They leave her no room to walk around or sit down. Despite the scene of oppression before you, Jurate welcomes you with a smile and heartfelt warmth. Then she invites you to dine with her. You agree, almost as if to humour her, and immediately, everything transforms.

The palace becomes whole and you and Jurate are seated in an opulent and extremely comfortable amber room, instead of in the midst of pieces of the broken palace. Jurate, now resplendent and seated on an amber throne, asks you what would you like to eat and drink and it magically appears before you. Jurate asks you if you would like music, and your favourite music begins to play. The food is delicious, the atmosphere, delightful.

When you and Jurate have finished with your refreshments, she asks you if you would like to play a game of shape-shift tag with her. You ask what it is and she tells you that it is like tag, but when you are touched you change into a different creature from the sea and continue in that form until tagged again. The object of the game is to get everyone frozen in a different form at once. You agree.

Jurate takes your hand and you both swim into a very large room, where five mermaids are waiting for you. Jurate rings a chime and the game begins. It is exhilarating to swim fast and change forms. All of the forms changed into are funny. Sometimes a mermaid changes and leaves her tail with a shark's head and things like that. You find that you get the hang of it right away. Everyone is playing this for fun and is supportive of each other. You play two rounds: one with Jurate as 'it' and the other with you as 'it'.

After the game Jurate thanks everyone. The mermaids leave. It feels time for you to leave and you tell Jurate. Immediately the palace transforms and you are standing next to Jurate who is heavily chained as before. You are puzzled about this situation and ask Jurate for clarification. Jurate tells you that what is imprisoned is her physical form or physical body. What cannot be imprisoned, unless she herself views prison as her reality, is her soul. Just like your physical body is someplace else resting while you have this experience with her. It is all about what you choose to focus on as your reality. You take this in on your deepest levels and understand it.

You thank Jurate and you walk around to the other side of the ruins, to where you came in. You easily find the opening of the tunnel and you enter.

Now you are going up, up, up, feeling clear and clean, refreshed and revitalized, up, up, up, with a deepening sense of peace, lots of space and quiet within, up, up, up, awake and aware, till you re-enter the cave. You walk out of the mouth of the cave and take a deep breath. As you release it you are back in your body. You take another deep breath and as you release it you are more present in your body and can move it gently. You take a last deep breath and as you exhale you may open your eyes.

Welcome back!
Take the time to journal!

Jurate's mythology is an excellent example of what I described in Chapter One under 'Herstory'. There seems to be two myths grafted together: one in which a goddess falls in love with a mortal man and another which is about the punishment meted out to women/goddesses who make their own choices. Jurate represents an older matrilineal culture that was supplanted by the newer patrilineal culture, in the personage of Perkunas. It tells the story of the changeover from a partnership society between women and men to the male dominator mode.

Mermaid Interlude: the Sea Lady

The Sea Lady was written by H.G. Wells in 1902. In this wonderful little book Mr Wells uses the device of Miss Waters, a mermaid, an alien being from a world vastly different from his own of early twentieth century Great Britain, to comment on and criticize the society of his time.

The Buntings were a respectable English family. They were middle class and proud of it. Mr Randolph Bunting derived his income in the trade of beer-making. This afforded the family the opportunity to take a house in Sandgate Castle, a fashionable summer seaside resort. Accompanying Mr and Mrs Bunting that August, were their three children: Fred, who worked with his father in the family business, his two sisters and their two guests the Miss Glendowers. The Miss Glendowers were half-sisters named Adeline and Mabel whom Mrs Bunting had taken upon herself to act in the capacity of a mother since their mother had died. Mabel was Fred's fiancée and Adeline, the heiress of the two, was engaged to Harry

Chatteris. He was an up and coming, brilliant and hand-some young politician, planning to run as Liberal candi-date in the next election.

Nephew of an earl, 'the hero of a scandal', Harry Chatteris had not a dime to his name. He was dependent on the good graces of an elderly aunt for his cash and she, approving of his engagement to the elder Miss Glendower, and his current choice of career, continued to keep him in good supply. Adeline for her part, was the sort of hard-working, serious, down-to-earth woman who recognized her life's work in Harry and promptly fell in love with what he could become with her help and money. Their engagement was satisfactory to both parties.

While Mabel and the Miss Buntings were swimming in the sea, they noticed a very fashionable and beautiful young lady appear to be swimming towards them. Suddenly the unknown lady disappeared under the water and a moment later one of her arms was seen flailing about. Immediately they all cried out for help and made for the shore. Mr Bunting and Fred answered their call and bare-ly managed to save the unknown lady without drowning themselves. The Lady wrapped her arms around Fred and he lifted her out of the sea and on to the shore.

Since all attention was focused on the safety of the Lady and the success of the rescue, no one noticed, as she was pulled out of the water, that she had a tail. The Lady herself told the small group that she had had a cramp and asked to be immediately brought into the Buntings' house, then fainted.

When they saw that the Lady was indeed different from themselves anatomically, and were certain that the difference was a tail and not an exotic bathing costume, it was too late to do anything about it. More people were coming to the beach to see what the excitement was all about. Although Mrs Bunting did think of tossing the Lady back into the sea, that would have involved detailed explanations, and so the mermaid was taken into their home.

Once situated in the Bunting home, the sea Lady appeals to Mrs Bunting's generous and maternal nature for help. She is an immortal and wants to acquire a soul and live like a normal human. Out of all the residents on this coast, she chose Mrs Bunting to live with as the best possible person to advise her. She is wanting to put herself completely under Mrs Bunting's care and be guided by her in everything. Finally, a small chest filled with gold and diamonds makes its appearance: the sea Lady is rich.

Mrs Bunting is persuaded to let the sea Lady stay as a paying guest and they both come up with a scheme to hide the fact that she is a mermaid. They will cover up the 'deformity', her tail, and tell people she is an invalid. Assured of her place in the Bunting home, the sea Lady accepts the suggested name, Miss Doris Waters, and inquires after a good dressmaker and maid.

Within a fortnight she is comfortably settled in the Bunting home, and manages to pass for a very reasonable human being of exceptional beauty, with large aquamarine eyes, blond hair done up in the latest fashion and lower body wrapped up as if injured. Mrs. Bunting is heard remarking, that 'although "they" will be as good as new, she'll never bicycle again.'

When Adeline discovers that Miss Waters will also be staying with the Buntings for the summer, she protests to Mrs Bunting. Adeline is concerned with the election coming up and all the work that needs to be done for Harry as candidate, that Miss Waters would just be in the way and divert the focus from Harry to herself. Mrs Bunting assures her that this will not be the case, but Adeline confesses that she doesn't trust the sea Lady. Mrs Bunting explains that she is here to get a soul, and even has meetings with the local clergyman. However, Adeline says she feels that Miss Waters is laughing at them all.

Harry arrives for a short stay and meets the charming Miss Waters. Captivated by her, he finds himself thrown together with her. He tells Melville, a mutual friend of his and the Buntings, about his regard for Miss Waters.

Soon after their chat, Melville finds himself alone at the house with Miss Waters. They engage in conversation and when Miss Waters asks with a great show of innocence about the relations between Chatteris and Miss

Glendower, Melville discovers her true purpose and confronts her with, 'It is him you came for.' And she confesses that it is.

The sea Lady tells Melville that she saw Harry years ago when he was in the South Seas and has never been able to get him out of her mind. Melville brings up the fact that he is engaged to Miss Glendower and Miss Waters makes light of that. Melville cries foul at that and states that she is an immortal and unencumbered and can do anything she likes, but humans cannot because of their short lives.

She confesses to him that the mer-folk watch the humans, sometimes with envy, but most of the time in amazement at the fears they have, the restrictions they put on themselves, the way humans limit and tie themselves in knots. 'Your life, I tell you, is a dream – a dream – and you can't wake out of it.'

'And if so, why do you tell me?'

'*Because*', she said, '*there are better dreams*.'[15]

Their talk is interrupted by the appearance of Mrs Bunting, who mistakes the tenor of their conversation. While seeing her friend off, she hints to him that the time to win Miss Waters is now or never. Melville flees to London and his club where he encounters a confused Chatteris who confides in him that he has decided not to run for election in Hythe. He is having second thoughts about devoting his whole life to politics. It seems absurd and no longer has meaning for him.

A week later Melville is urgently summoned to help in a crisis by Mrs Bunting. Upon arriving in Sandgate, he is told that Miss Waters has seduced Harry, and Harry has broken off the engagement with Adeline. The sea Lady was asked to leave and now lives at the hotel in town. Harry is staying at another hotel in town. Mrs Bunting dispatches Melville to see Harry and fix it all up. Before he can go, Adeline asks for a conference. She explains that Harry has written to her and wants to come back to her, but he hasn't come to see her yet. She urges him to tell Harry that she loves him and wants him back. All he needs to do is come to her.

Harry knows that being with Adeline is the right thing for him to do, the sane thing, the most reasonable thing, and states he never realized how splendid a woman she is until now. When Melville asks the question, if he will go back to her, Harry gives him an enthusiastic yes.

When their conversation turns to the sea Lady, it is clear that Harry is stuck vacillating between the two. Adeline represents duty and reason and Miss Waters represents passion, romance and the unknown, each is the opposite of the other. When Melville encourages Harry to call on Adeline now, tonight, he assures him that he will call on Adeline, only not tonight, a night of such magic. Tomorrow is the right time to visit Adeline: in the clear light of a grey day. But that is not to be.

At some point during the night, Harry shaves, changes his clothes and goes to Miss Waters' hotel, where he demands to see her. Her maid prepares her and Harry rushes up to be with her.

A little while later, they are both seen leaving the hotel and heading for the beach; she in his arms, triumphant, wearing a light robe and with her hair loose and shimmering. They enter the water and are seen no more.

During his morning shift, a policeman comes across the brand new discarded robe and wonders why anyone would throw away something as useful as a good robe.

Mermaid power snack!

When we think of or attend the 'power breakfast' it is usually not about food but about who we are dining with. Here is a delectable treat that allows you to have your power and eat it, too! This recipe harnesses the potency of the mermaids, through your charging – which, as we know by now, means raising focused energy in your body and then directing it into what you are holding – the ingredients. The mermaid cakes can be served for breakfast or a tea break. And it will change the meaning of the power breakfast to a breakfast that empowers you!

Mermaid cakes

(makes 1 dozen cakes)

INGREDIENTS

450g/1lb organic wholemeal pastry flour
6 tablespoons baking powder
450g/1lb organic rolled oats
225g/8oz organic raw butter, or organic butter, softened
225g/8oz organic goat milk or organic raw milk
4 large organic free-range eggs
225g/8oz dulse seaweed
1 teaspoon celtic sea salt or organic salt

PREPARATION

1. Do the **Ritual for Charging Objects** on page 30
2. Preheat the oven to 175°C/350°F degrees and prepare to play.
3. Mix the flour with the baking powder and salt, while thinking joyful thoughts.
4. Toss in the oats. Tell them you love them.

5. Cut in the butter, while 'cutting a small rug.' ('Cutting a rug' means to dance.)

6. Whip the milk and eggs together, while adding some delight.

7. When the flour mixture is coarse, stir in the milk and eggs, and sing your favourite song as if you were an opera diva.

8. Put the dulse in a strainer and run water over it until it is entirely wet and softens enough to shred. Shred or cut the dulse in small pieces and mix with the batter. Sing an imitation of your favourite singer or group.

9. Take a greased baking sheet and drop the batter onto the sheet making 12 mounds. You can wet your hands and shape the cakes if needed. Put in the oven for 30–45 minutes, or until they are done. They should be a pale colour.

10. Take out and serve with butter.

Now that the cakes are done, don't stop the magic! Make a mini ritual of eating your mermaid cakes.

Mini ritual for mermaid cakes

1. Chew slowly and enjoy the taste of mermaid empowerment in each bite.
2. Feel, sense or see your body, mind and spirit becoming filled with more energy and vitality.
3. Notice the difference as all your senses are heightened.
4. Take time to savour the sheer pleasure of eating, and to give that pleasure to your whole body.
5. Are you steamed up and ready for action? Good. Get on with your life!

All mermaids are savvy about prosperity. They do live in the ocean, after all, which is the most abundant of natural resources. Whether it's old treasure from sunken ships or pearls, coral and amber, these witchy water babes have secrets to share!

CHAPTER 5

Mermaid Magic for Prosperity & Life Purpose

Oh the joy of developing a good tight relationship with our fabulous mermaid friends. Now they are ready to reveal all and allow us access to their most cherished secrets: those of prosperity and life purpose.

The sweetness of life

We live in an abundant world where so much is possible and more becomes possible daily. Just think how fortunate you are to be able to go into a store and buy this book or receive it as a gift. That in itself is a simple act of magic. One hundred years ago books were costly. Two hundred years ago and you might not have been taught how to read. By viewing life with perspective we can come to appreciate all that we have. And by recognizing and acknowledging the bounty already in our lives we can create more. **The seeds that we need to plant to reap our share of prosperity are gratitude and appreciation**.

How often do you taste and enjoy the sweetness that is life, just the simple fact that you are living and experiencing in this unique human body? Do you make time to stop and smell the roses? Or are you, as an acquaintance once remarked, too busy selling them? Do you live each day overflowing with gratitude for all you have? Or do you live your life as if you are on starvation rations? Are you harvesting the full abundance that is in your life? Or are you reaping your thoughts of lack?

'Enough stressing about money!', the mermaids sing in my ear. 'Life is to be enjoyed and lived to the fullest. You humans worry too much. If you live the gift that is life, you will be gifted and your life will be a gift.' They are right. And to fully capture our attention and awaken our sensuous sides, they invite you to stop, slow down and experience the richness of life through some of your strongest senses, that of taste, smell and sound, in their next offering and ritual.

It's merrily off to the kitchen we go to tantalize our taste buds with a couple of mouth-watering desserts, and then we will be incorporating (eating!) these in the Ritual for Sweetness.

Tropical Mermaid Pudding

Serves 4–5

A favourite with mermaids of South America, the Caribbean, Hawaii and Indonesia!

INGREDIENTS

- *115g/4oz dried Irish moss*
- *2 cans organic coconut milk (can size: 400ml/14–15fl oz)*
- *115g/4oz organic succanet, or,*
- *55g/2oz raw honey*
- *pinch of celtic sea salt or organic salt*
- *115g/4oz organic dried coconut – optional*
- *your favourite dance music*

INSTRUCTIONS

1. Put on your music and get your energy moving and shaking.
2. While dancing, breathe love in and out from your heart chakra.

3. Pick up the ingredients and dance them around the room.

4. Soak the Irish moss in water for 15 minutes.

5. Assemble a double boiler by filling the bottom saucepan with water and putting the second saucepan on top. Bring the bottom saucepan to a boil, then combine the coconut milk with succanet (or if you are using honey, wait until step 7) in the top saucepan.

6. Strain the moss and add to the coconut milk mixture and cook over boiling water for 25 minutes. Occasionally stir in love and delight.

7. Strain the milk mixture to remove the seaweed. Add raw honey if you are using it instead of succanet and thoroughly blend with the milk mixture, then add the organic dried coconut, if using. Add salt. Stir the mixture and pour into individual dessert cups. Chill and serve.

For decadent mermaids who-love-chocolate-too-much, here is an alternative recipe that will be just as successful in awakening your sensual side during the ritual on page 183:

Suntanned Tropical Mermaid Pudding

INGREDIENTS

Same ingredients as the Tropical Mermaid Pudding with the addition of:

◆ *115g/4oz of your favourite hot chocolate mix, preferably organic, that is pre-sweetened.*

INSTRUCTIONS

Follow the instructions in the recipe for the Tropical Mermaid Pudding above, and add the hot chocolate mix to the coconut milk mixture in step 5.

Now that we've concocted these succulent confections it is time to revel in them to the fullest with our next delectable ritual.

WARNING: The following ritual can transform your relationship with food forever!

Ritual of sweetness

1. Light a candle.

2. Surround yourself with white light by envisioning yourself inside a luminous egg.

3. Breathe love in and out of your heart chakra.

4. Take a taste of the pudding. Chew it slowly. Notice the full flavour. Taste the coconut oil in the pudding. Appreciate how rich and delectable it is. Allow it to float through your mouth. Feel it tickle the pleasure centres in your taste buds. Now send that pleasure through your body. Breathe in this moment of enjoyment, life's sweetness.

5. Take another mouthful and do the same with the rest of your serving of pudding.

6. You will know that you have done this ritual successfully, if you feel completely satiated when you finish your pudding and feel aglow with the joy of living.

7. Give thanks to the mermaids.
8. Blow out your candle and get on with your day.

A sacred marriage within

According to Jungian thought man has an inner woman, the **anima**, which he needs to be in good relationship with to have successful relations to the women in his life and to his inner world or spirituality. Jung's term for the inner man in women is the **animus**. Woman needs to cultivate the right relationship with her animus to have successful relations with the men in her life and in her ability to manifest in the outside world. Success, happiness and prosperity for women, then, is about being in partnership with her animus. One way of achieving this is to make what ancients and alchemists referred to as the Hieros Gamos, or inner marriage of the masculine and feminine.

Water mother **Mere-Ama** insisted She be included in *Mermaid Magic*! Who was I to argue with a goddess? She wants to help you with fertility and abundance. She also knows how to have a good time at a party, as you will see when you journey to her after this pause for a Mythological Moment.

Mythological Moment: Mere-Ama

To the Finns, Mere-Ama was the goddess prayed to for fertility and abundance. She was also the very spirit of water residing in brooks, streams, lakes – any body of water, including the ocean. A wise and loving 'mature' mermaid with long silver- and white-striped hair, whose favourite drink was brandy, Mere-Ama was always gifted with generous libations to guarantee an abundant supply of fish. After the wedding, when a new wife took up residence in her husband's home, she would be sure to go to a body of water nearby to introduce herself to the 'water mother' Mere-Ama. Finnish women knew that their gifts of food and clothing would always ensure that they gave birth to healthy children.

Mere-Ama was considered so much a part of the life of her people, that when people got married when the water was frozen, they would repeat the festivities when the water had thawed and were sure Mere-Ama could join them.

Journey to Mere-Ama

Find a time and a place when and where you will not be disturbed. Sit, lie or stand with your spine straight and close your eyes. Surround yourself with white light by envisioning yourself inside a luminous egg. Take a deep breath and release it with a sigh. Take another deep breath and release it with a moan. Take a last deep breath and release it with a snake-like hiss. Let your breathing return to normal.

See, sense or feel the entrance to a cave. It can be a cave that you know or one that exists in your imagination. Take a deep breath and as you exhale, stand at the mouth of the cave. Put your hand on the cave's opening. What does it feel like? Now enter the cave.

The cave is a good size, comfortably warm and well lit. You walk to the back of the cave and notice that it becomes a tunnel. You enter the tunnel and go down, down, down. Deeper and deeper and deeper. Down, down, down. Becoming more relaxed, letting go, going deeper. Down, down, down. Deeper and deeper and deeper. Until you reach the end where you see some different coloured light. On the count of three you will step out into the otherworld. One – two – three. Step out of the tunnel.

You hear the sounds of a rustic orchestra tuning up and you see people dressed up festively in their folk costumes. You are at a wedding party taking place beside a large lake. In your arms is a beautiful dress. You are carrying the dress of the guest of honour, Mere-Ama. You take it to the water to throw it in. Right after you do, a woman approaches the lake with a full bottle of liquor, which she pours into the water, chanting the name 'Mere-Ama'.

You join the woman in her chant in front of the lake. The chant is taken up by the rest of the party. You hear a cry of 'there she is', then you see Mere-Ama rise out of the water wearing the dress you brought. She joins the people on the land and signals to the orchestra to begin.

They play a slow, moving tune and Mere-Ama grabs your right hand. Another guest takes your left hand. The whole group dances in a circle dance (dance that is done usually by joining hands and dancing in a circle), with the movements of a deliberate, specific invitation: that of calling in your animus. The steps are simple and at times the dance moves into the circle, then out of the circle, and then around in a circle. This time, when you go into the centre of the circle and come out again, a man appears in the centre. He seems familiar to you and then again, completely unknown. The dance ends and he comes over to you and asks you to join him in the centre.

You agree and the circle of people applaud. Then you notice that he is wearing the clothes of a groom and you are now dressed in the clothes of a bride. Mere-Ama brings you a bridal headdress. She tells you that you are here to make the sacred marriage within and that the man in the centre is your animus. She performs the ceremony and when she is finished you feel married to your inner man.

The next circle dance is a dance that evokes the fertility of life which is brought about by the pairing of the masculine and feminine dynamics. You and your animus dance the dance, which is a dance of women and men weaving together. The following circle dance is one that speaks of the web of all life, the connections of humans, animals, earth, death and rebirth, taking care of each other and the land. The music is stirring and the combination of dancing outside in the sunlight, with a live orchestra, with people who know the dance and use it to celebrate life, brings you to a state of ecstasy. You are one with everyone there, with your animus, with the web of life and your part in it, with the day and with Mere-Ama. You feel you now know your place in life and it is good.

The last circle dance is one of closing. Of taking the energy raised in the dancing and sending it out in the world for humanity, and of taking it into your heart to assist you on your own life's path. The dance ends with the men merging into the women in the circle, including you and your animus. Now there are only women left in the circle. You are feeling deeply transformed, peaceful, whole. When the music ends, Mere-Ama thanks you for coming. You thank her for inviting you. You easily find the opening of the tunnel and you enter.

Now you are going up, up, up, feeling clear and clean, refreshed and revitalized, up, up, up, with a deepening sense of peace, lots of space and quiet within, up, up, up, awake and aware, till you re-enter the cave. You walk out of the mouth of the cave and take a deep breath. As you release it you are back in your body. You take another deep breath and as you release it you are more present in your body and can move it gently. You take a last deep breath and as you exhale you may open your eyes.

Welcome back!

Now that you've returned, this is a good time to write in your journal about your experiences while journeying.

Mermaid Interlude: Johnny Croy and his mermaid bride

This folktale comes from the Orkney Islands in Scotland, a land rich in selkie tales.

There was a man, a handsome bonny man by the name of Johnny Croy, of Volyar in Orkney. Oh he was a fine man, was he, but a bit full of himself for many a pretty lass of the neighbourhood set her cap for him, but he'd give her never a glance at all. A hard worker was Johnny, who loved all the animals on his farm, did he. He was never in debt and always willing to help those less fortunate.

One day while gathering up some seaweed for his mother on the west side of Sanday, he was astonished by the most beautiful voice he had ever heard singing a delicate tasteful tune. It stopped him cold, it did, and he felt a strong urge to find out who the singer was.

Tiptoeing around a large boulder, he found the wee singer, and lo to his amazement when he discovered who it was. It was a mermaid singing as she combed her glistening mane of bright gold hair.

Now some might have run from the sight, but not our Johnny. No not he. He decided right then and there that he would have her and only she for a wife. So he crept up behind her and put his arms around her and gave her a pretty kiss. She stood right up and gave him a blow that knocked him down on the rocks. Then, quick as lightning she sped down to the water and dove into the sea.

Johnny noticed something glistening on the rock and saw that she had left her wee golden comb in her haste. He picked it up and ran down to the water's edge. She was watching him, thinking, what a bold handsome man and feeling torn between anger for being rudely accosted and love for the look of him. Then she saw that he had her comb and she begged him to give it back.

He said he'd give it back to her if she would wed him and live with him on land. 'I have a large house with a good farm with cows and sheep. You'll never be wanting for anything in your life and you'll be mistress of all.'

But the mermaid said no. 'You come with me to live under the sea. We shall live in a crystal palace where the weather will never freeze us or the wind bite us.'

Each tried to tempt the other and the more they tried the more deeply they loved, till the mermaid, who went by the name of Gem-de-Lovely, saw people coming and turned and swam out to sea. There was nothing more for Johnny to do but to take his love-sick heart home.

Now his mother was a wise woman who knew all sorts of healing ways. When he told her what had happened, how he would never love another, she railed at him for his foolishness. 'If you want my advice, throw that comb into the sea; but you'll not take it, for all men are fools when it comes to love.' But he would have none of that. So she told him to keep that treasure hidden and the mermaid would come to him for it is her most precious treasure. 'There's only one I can save and I know it is not you.'

Johnny hid the comb and went back to his work. But his heart wasn't in it and he had trouble sleeping. Then one night Gem-de-Lovely appeared at the foot of his bed. 'My bonnie love, I must have my comb. Will you come live with me in the sea?'

'Nay, that I cannot. Will you not consent to live with me on land before my heart breaks,' said Johnny.

'I will marry you if after seven years of life with you on land, you and all that is mine will come to live with me in the sea.'

Johnny could not say yes fast enough and he swore an oath to keep his word. On their wedding day the bride was clearly uneasy in the kirk (Scottish church) and stuffed her golden hair in her ears when there was praying, but that went unremarked because of her bonnie beauty, with her decked out in a gold and silver dress and necklace of enormous pearls.

Gem-de-Lovely made Johnny a good wife and they loved each other well. Seven bairns did they have, each weaned at Granny Croy's own little house with the youngest in his crib near Granny's own bed. As the eve of the day ending the seven years approached, Gem-de-Lovely began a great packing, as if they were leaving for a long voyage. On the night of the last day, Granny took the cross she kept on her altar and put it in the fire till it was red hot, then she branded the youngest babe on his backside.

A large boat arrived and the servants of Gem-de-Lovely's folk came and packed up the family. All were assembled on the beach; Gem-de-Lovely, as radiant and well-dressed as a queen, and Johnny Croy, her bonnie man, with their six children. Granny Croy sat before them on a rock nearby. Gem-de-Lovely sent her servants for her youngest babe, but they came back being unable to lift the cradle. She ran up to the house herself, but when she tried to take her babe in her arms, she shrieked with pain, and lifting up the blankets, saw the cross on his flesh.

Moaning over having to leave her youngest, she returned to the ship and set sail. Johnny and his family were never seen in Orkney again.

Granny Croy brought the babe up and named him Corsa Croy (Croy of the Cross). Corsa Croy did deeds that brought him fame and his fame brought him great wealth. He married a nobleman's daughter, had many bairns and lived a long, healthy and lucky life, thanks, in part, to his mermaid blood.

Eating with gratitude

There is something deeply satisfying about combining food preparation and eating with prosperity. A knowing that slumbers in our cells. In ancient times, before money was invented, the measure of wealth was grain and live-stock, items that were used for food. A city was rich if it had numerous stores of grain and huge flocks and herds. It is this old resonance of combining food with prosperity and abundance that echos in the journey and ritual of our next mermaid goddess, **Benten**.

Mythological Moment: Benten

Benten swims through the Sea of Japan to visit her many shrines, either in the shape of a dragon, or with the top-half a beautiful woman, lower-half dragon or fish. This Japanese Sea Goddess is popular with those needing help in their romantic, intellectual or artistic endeavours. For those who petition her for assistance in the financial arena, she brings the blessings of abundance.

The only female among the seven gods of good luck, Benten is said to resemble the Hindu goddess of the arts, the pursuit of knowledge and good luck, Saraswati, and like her, she is often depicted with eight arms. Benten's sacred animal is the snake and her favourite stones are jade and pearls.

Benten acquired her attribute of 'protector of children' when she wed the great dragon who was regularly eating the children of Koshigoe. The marriage changed the drag-on's dietary preferences and the grateful people honoured Benten. In a similar mythological vein, Benten stopped the earthquakes caused by unruly underground serpents when she mated with them in her dragon form.

And now we are off to the exotic orient for a powerful prosperity journey with the good luck mermaid goddess, Benten.

Journey to Benten

Find a time and a place when and where you will not be disturbed. Sit, lie or stand with your spine straight and close your eyes. Surround yourself with white light by envisioning yourself inside a luminous egg. Take a deep breath and release it with a sigh. Take another deep breath and release it with a moan. Take a last deep breath and release it with a snake-like hiss. Let your breathing return to normal.

See, sense or feel the entrance to a cave. It can be a cave that you know or one that exists in your imagination. Take a deep breath and as you exhale, stand at the mouth of the cave. Put your hand on the cave's opening. What does it feel like? Now enter the cave.

The cave is a good size, comfortably warm and well lit. You walk to the back of the cave and notice that it becomes a tunnel. You enter the tunnel and go down, down, down. Deeper and deeper and deeper. Down, down, down. Becoming more relaxed, letting go, going deeper. Down, down, down. Deeper and deeper and deeper. Until you reach the end where you see some different coloured light. On the count of three you will step out into the otherworld. One – two – three. Step out of the tunnel.

You are standing on a beach and can see a small rocky island with a shrine on it. The tide is low and you walk over to the island. Once on the island, you head for the entryway of the shrine. You see a bell-pull and you clap your hands together twice and then pull the bell twice, chanting: 'O Benten Mikami'. You hear sounds of someone coming, and Benten walks out of the shrine to greet you.

You bow to her and she answers your bow with another bow. Then she guides you into her shrine, to a large *tatami* (woven straw mat) room which overlooks the sea.

Benten sits on the *tatami* and asks you to sit down, and you do so. She asks you why you have come to see her. You tell her you are needing her assistance with prosperity. She smiles and agrees to help you.

Benten picks up her *biwa* (Japanese mandolin) and begins playing a lively tune. Her music is so stirring that you find yourself dancing to Benten's playing. Dancing as you have never danced before in your life. You are dancing in ways that evoke the core of your being, your full authentic self. You are dancing your joy, your playfulness, carefree as a child. Stepping and stomping and whirling and twirling. Feeling completely safe and comfortable to show yourself in dance.

When you have danced all that is appropriate for you, both you and Benten finish together. Benten bows to you and you bow to her. Benten invites you to sit down again and you now notice there is a table on the mats between you and Benten, with bowls filled with something steaming.

You sit down and sniff the bowl. It smells like the sea. Benten tells you that this is her secret recipe. She calls it 'Benten's Bounty' and asks you to try it. And you do so. It is delicious and deeply nourishing.

You ask Benten what is in it and she tells you it is not only the ingredients but the way you prepare it and the way you eat it that brings prosperity. You take pure water and give thanks for the water. You take two different kinds of seaweed and give thanks to the seaweed. You take shitake mushrooms and give thanks to the mushrooms. If you decide to use miso, you give thanks to the miso. And when you eat it you say: *'Thank you pure water. Thank you kelp and alaria. Thank you shitake. Thank you miso. Your life and my life. One life in gratitude.'*

As you eat and drink the soup, you feel extremely grateful. You feel privileged to live the life you do. Thankful for everything in it. Accepting of what comes your way. You feel you have entered into a state of grace. And are so filled with peace that you and Benten sit and finish your soup in silence.

After a while, you look out at the sea and notice that

the tide is returning. You thank Benten and stand up. Benten stands and you both bow. You walk out of the shrine. You walk back to the mainland and easily find the opening of the tunnel and you enter.

Now you are going up, up, up, feeling clear and clean, refreshed and revitalized, up, up, up, with a deepening sense of peace, lots of space and quiet within, up, up, up, awake and aware, till you re-enter the cave. You walk out of the mouth of the cave and take a deep breath. As you release it you are back in your body. You take another deep breath and as you release it you are more present in your body and can move it gently. You take a last deep breath and as you exhale you may open your eyes.

Welcome back!

Journal time!

Prepare yourself for another double-duty treat in the following ritual! Not only will the 'Benten's Bounty' recipe raise your gratitude quotient and assist you in manifesting prosperity, but this scrumptious soup is an immune-system booster and will protect you from cancer!

'Benten's Bounty' ritual

(serves 1)

INGREDIENTS

+ *55g/2oz alaria seaweed cut up into 2.5cm/1 inch pieces*
+ *55g/2oz digitata (kombu) seaweed cut up into 2.5cm/1 inch pieces*
+ *500ml/16fl oz spring water or filtered water*
+ *4–8 dried shitake mushrooms broken into small pieces*
+ *1 teaspoon–1 tablespoon organic dark unpasteurized miso (optional)*

INSTRUCTIONS

1. Put the seaweed in a stainless steel pot and add the spring or filtered water. Bring to boil, then gently simmer for 10 minutes with the lid on.
2. Add the shitake mushrooms, replace the lid and continue to simmer for 30 minutes.
3. Pour into a bowl to serve and add the miso (if using).
4. Now say the following: *'Thank you pure water.*

Thank you kombu and alaria. Thank you shitake. Thank you miso. Your life and my life. One life in gratitude.'

5.   Now you are ready to eat and enjoy your soup.

Mermaid travel tips

What better way to celebrate your prosperity than to make a pilgrimage to your favourite mermaid goddess to thank Her for Her abundant assistance. There is nothing like travelling for gaining a true appreciation of all that is in your life. If you are interested in being part of a yearly festival or ceremony, then it would be best to time your visit to the dates of Yemanja's and Benten's festivals.

Yemanja's festival is in Brazil, Rio Vermelho Beach, Bahia, and it is on February 2. It is a big affair with hundreds of celebrants. You will need to pack white clothes or purchase them there – even better, as they sell beautiful things at reasonable prices.

Plan your trip to Japan in the summer near the solstice for Benten's festival. You can visit the Temple in the centre of Shinabazu Pond in Ueno, in the huge sprawling city of Tokyo, or find Benten Island, a little rocky outcropping in which a Benten-sama is set up, just off the coast of Japan.

You might like to get your tail done in time to attend and take part in the Annual Coney Island Mermaid Parade, just outside of New York City, USA, at the beginning of summer. This event is filled with razzle-dazzle and draws huge crowds.

To commune with the most ancient of mermaid goddesses, Britomartis, you will need to go to Crete, the town of Elounda (or Elouda) in the Lasithi prefecture, Greece. There you will enjoy the peaceful and rejuvenating effects of the lagoon, believed to be still inhabited by the goddess.

To visit any of the other mermaid goddesses listed in the book, just look up their country of origin and do a search on-line and you will get a fix on their location in order to plan your visit. Bon voyage!

Moving our focus now to our life's purpose, we will consort with our phenomenal immortal mer-friends to whip up a luscious life, and gain their magical assistance in finding and living our life's unique purpose.

Finding your life purpose

We come into this life as a complete unknown. We are the jungles we need to enter, we are the watery deeps howling for exploration, we are the planets, stars and solar systems waiting to be probed and named. The greatest discoveries we can make in our lifetime is in knowing who we are and what our purpose is.

Why is purpose so important? Because it creates direction, a star by which to orient our lives, and it makes life manageable through the guidance that the purpose becomes. **The best way to find your life's purpose is through discovering your bliss**.

Fortunately for us followers of 'the Mermaid Philosophy of Life', which is to have the absolute best time and create a life filled with magic and love and fun, we are open to learning what we love to do, what ignites and inspires us, what makes us happy. We have experienced the power of love and delight. We say YES to bliss, knowing that as we recover and live our bliss, our joy radiates out to the world and our lives become its greatest blessing. And salvation.

To aid us in our quest is our Inner Mermaid, our wild feminine part, where all that knowledge still lives and breathes, swims and plays. The last mermaid goddess to grace this book, **Amphitrite**, will also be giving us a helping hand.

Mythological Moment: Amphitrite

An ancient pre-Hellenic Triple Goddess whose name means 'all encircling Triad', which is the sea that surrounds the earth. When Amphitrite walked about on her queendom, the waters grew calm and still. She is referred to by the Greek poet Pindar as 'Amphitrite, goddess of the golden spindle', and other references speak of her singing and dancing. Known as Salacia to the Romans, so entwined is her surviving mythology with her husband, Poseidon to the Greeks or Neptune to the Romans, that when depicted in art she never appears without him.

Amphitrite did not want to marry Poseidon, one of the upstart newcomer Patriarchial Greeks. She flatly refused him when he first proposed. After all, she was THE sea goddess and ruled her kingdom perfectly well without a man, thank you. However, the dolphin Delphinus, who found where she had fled from Poseidon's unwanted attentions, managed to persuade her to marry the god. The dolphin's reward was being placed in the sky as a constellation. Amphitrite's was being demoted from great Triple Goddess to a mere nymph.

We will now enter the watery realm of the Great Triple Goddess, Amphitrite, but before we do, let's make sure we are all on the same page. In this next journey we will be asked to align our personality/ego with our soul. What this means is that you will be taking your everyday consciousness or the aspect of you that is your daily awareness and merging it with your soul, which is a higher aspect of your consciousness. As you may remember, the soul is where the blueprint for this life is stored. Right then, let's not keep Amphitrite waiting!

Journey to Amphitrite

Find a time and a place when and where you will not be disturbed. Sit, lie or stand with your spine straight and close your eyes. Surround yourself with white light by envisioning yourself inside a luminous egg. Take a deep breath and release it with a sigh. Take another deep breath and release it with a moan. Take a last deep breath and release it with a snake-like hiss. Let your breathing return to normal.

See, sense or feel the entrance to a cave. It can be a cave that you know or one that exists in your imagination. Take a deep breath and as you exhale, stand at the mouth of the cave. Put your hand on the cave's opening. What does it feel like? Now enter the cave.

The cave is a good size, comfortably warm and well lit. You walk to the back of the cave and notice that it becomes a tunnel. You enter the tunnel and go down, down, down. Deeper and deeper and deeper. Down, down, down. Becoming more relaxed, letting go, going deeper. Down, down, down. Deeper and deeper and deeper. Until you reach the end where you see some different coloured light. On the count of three you will step out into the otherworld. One – two – three. Step out of the tunnel.

You are on the beach of the Mediterranean Sea. You walk down to the shore to sit on the sand. The sea is very rough, huge waves swell and it looks like it will storm. As you gaze out across the ocean, you notice a chariot drawn by white horses coalescing out of the surf. The figure in the chariot is Amphitrite in her young maid aspect, and as soon as she appears, the sun comes out and the sea becomes calm. She rides her chariot right up to you, then jumps down and asks you if you would like to come to her palace at the bottom of the sea. You say yes and she helps you on to the chariot. Then she takes the reins, turns the horses around and you all drive into the sea.

As soon as everyone is submerged in the water, the chariot and horses disappear and you and Amphitrite transform into mermaids and begin swimming. Soon you arrive at the palace. It is made from all the treasures of the sea.

Amphitrite swims into the palace and you follow. There are many lovely rooms with exotic weavings hung.

You ask her about the weavings and she tells you they are hers. Then she takes you into a large room with a golden spinning wheel and loom. She seats herself by the loom and focuses her hands over the loom. It begins to work itself, at a very high speed. Soon there is a piece of cloth. Amphitrite beckons you over to look. You see images woven in the cloth, telling a story. There is a picture of you sitting on the shore and then one of Amphitrite in her chariot, then with the two of you in the chariot, then both of you in mermaid form swimming, and finally Amphitrite at her loom with you watching.

The Sea Goddess explains that this is a magic loom that can enable the weaver to create her life from her bliss. She tells you that everyone who is born comes to live on the earth with a special gift to give. It is when people discover that gift and give it that they feel blissful. Then she asks you if you want to discover your gift. You say yes and you exchange places with Amphitrite. She tells you that it is very easy and that she will guide you to do it.

'Take a breath and as you release it bring stillness to your physical body. Take a breath and as you release it bring peace to your emotional body. Take a breath and as you release it bring serenity to your mental body. See, sense or feel your soul. Now align your personality with your soul. It can be a sense of lifting up and holding a higher tension.

'Now float the question: what is my gift? Wait until you feel an answer coming and place your hands over the loom. Just let the energy flow. Whatever comes in response to your question. Keep holding on to the response to your question for as long as is appropriate for you, keeping your hands over the loom, until you feel done. Then relax your hands.

'Take a deep breath and bring your focus to your heart.'

Amphitrite brings you your material. The colours, images, textures and sense of the weaving reflects exactly what you have experienced as your gift. You are pleased. Amphitrite takes the material and shakes it out, and magically the material becomes a vest. She tells you to put it on and you do. Immediately you feel a deeper sense of clarity and focus. A strong sense of direction. It is a bit like a rebirth or an awakening. And you feel wonderful.

Struck by the simplicity of what you now know, you begin laughing and Amphitrite joins you. It is time now, to return, and you thank Amphitrite. She asks you for a gift and you give it to her with an open heart.

She takes your hand and you swim out of the palace with her. She calls her chariot and horses and they appear and you both take your places. Soon the horses break through to the surface of the ocean and you and Amphitrite are transformed back into fully human figures. After a short, fast ride across the top of the water, you are brought back to the beach. After watching Amphitrite leave, you easily find the opening of the tunnel and enter.

Now you are going up, up, up, feeling clear and clean, refreshed and revitalized, up, up, up, with a deepening sense of peace, lots of space and quiet within, up, up, up, awake and aware, till you re-enter the cave. You walk out of the mouth of the cave and take a deep breath. As you release it you are back in your body. You take another deep breath and as you release it you are more present in your body and can move it gently. You take a last deep breath and as you exhale you may open your eyes.

Welcome back!

Take some time to journal all that you discovered during your journey. You might want to draw or paint or dance or sing the energetic of what you discovered is your gift. Keep your discovery close to your chest; let it live in you and grow strong before you share it with the world.

Creating a joyful life!

Your life's purpose is what you came into this incarnation to do. The ways that you choose to manifest that can change as you engage in life. Our predominant cultural paradigm, however, offers only one template for a successful life: a life-long career in which you start at the bottom and work your way to the top, get married and have children. Rather than taking this for your model, dare to create your life according to what brings you the greatest joy! When you do this, then you are living the wisdom of the mermaids.

Here are a couple of fun activities to create a visual reminder of all that we've learned from the mermaids, in ways that will bring all those benefits into our daily life.

Mermaid life-map collage

I am sure you have heard of making life-map collages. They have been used for bringing in anything from love to prosperity to the right job to a fabulous home. Now that you have experienced *Mermaid Magic* this is the ideal time for you to take the knowledge you've acquired and put it in a life map for yourself.

How the mermaid life-map collage is different from the other life-maps is that this life map, besides having pictures of mermaids, has pictures or symbols representing your bliss and how you will live your gift. It is not about what you need to acquire but how you need to experience life on a daily basis. You are making a map of your bliss to use as a reminder.

For example: my life's purpose is to radiate love and light. Ways that I do this are through daily meditation, writing books, singing, dancing, cooking, being with my cats, living in community. So on my mermaid life map are pictures: of a brilliant sunset, which to me symbolizes radiating light; a goddess meditating (Kuan Yin – who reminds me of compassion); a rose quartz – which I equate with love; the Yemanja card from my first book and deck, *The Goddess Oracle*; bits of love poetry; photos of my cats, and so on. You get the picture.

WHAT YOU WILL NEED ...

✦ *scissors*
✦ *a large sheet of cardboard – this is what you will be pasting your pictures on so choose the size that will work for you*
✦ *pictures, pictures, pictures – from old calendars, on-line, magazines, and so on*
✦ *non-toxic, environmentally-safe glue*
✦ *magic markers or pens if you want to use words*
✦ *music that you love*

Close your door, unplug the telephone, put on your music and create.

'Mermaid Philosophy of Life' reminder

By now, after our deep, satisfying swim through this book, we are perfectly drenched and wringing wet in mermaid philosophy. Since we all could do with a little reminder, something to put on our refrigerator or bathroom wall, or next to our computer screen, or tattooed and embellished with mermaids on our skin (just joking!), here is a summation of the main points of the philosophy, direct and to the point, for your designing pleasure.

1. **Love yourself**
2. **Engage your senses**
3. **Do at least one fun thing a day**
4. **Surround yourself with music**
5. **Expect magic to happen**
6. **Live as if you are an immortal** (which is what the mermaids are)

7. In the words of Miss Waters, our mermaid source of power from *The Sea Lady* from Chapter 4, live your life daily with the knowledge that '**There are better dreams**'. You don't have to settle for a narrow life filled with worry, fear and proscribed by cultural norms.

There are many ways you can create your reminder. You can design it on your computer using one fabulous font; you can sew it on a piece of material; you can write it on the wall of your bedroom, or you can make tee-shirts.

Parting words

I hope you have enjoyed reading this book as much as I have delighted in its creation. The mermaids are sensational beings. If you take the time to connect with them, they will assist you in transforming your life. I wish you the most fabulous life that you can envision for yourself.

Mermaids and Lunar Magic

Now that we know what lunar magic is (see Chapter 2), here is a list of the meanings of the astrological signs, along with their corresponding mermaid goddess and invocations.

The invocations here can be used, or treated as a source of inspiration for your own verbal magic. And, they can be incorporated into any and all lunar magic rituals, if you so desire.

Remember, all you need for lunar magic is a clear intent for what you want to create with your magic and a calendar with the phases of the moon, along with a listing of when the moon is in what sign.

Moon in Aries

(Element: Fire)

This is a good time to begin anything. Ruled by the fiery, impulsive Aries, you will be raring to go and get anything you choose to do started. It is also an excellent time to centre on letting your unique individuality shine. For healing, focus on the head or begin an exercise regime. Projects that are begun during the moon in Aries have the energy to get off the ground.

Britomartis agrees to be evocable for Moon in Aries magic. She is THE mermaid of selfhood; the one who is virgin – whole and complete unto herself.

Oh shining sweet one
Come
protectress and huntress
of the wild
Come down from your high place
Come in from your sea depths

I invite you to be with me now
Here I have created your altar
Here I have brought you your favourite things
O shining sweet one
Britomartis
Come.
[Wait for Her to arrive]
I give thanks
She is here.

Moon in Taurus

(Element: Earth)

As Taurus is called the 'money sign of the zodiac', this is the best time to work prosperity magic. This can also be an excellent time to create anything you want to be long lasting, or to call stability into your life. Since Venus is ruling Taurus you may be given extra assistance in working romance rituals. For healing, focus on the throat and cerebellum (the back part of the brain).

Amphitrite, the weaving mermaid goddess, will work wonders with you when the moon is in Taurus.

Sea maid
Sea mother
Sea crone
I bow to you
I sing to you
I speak the words of respect
and praise
You who are the bounty of the ocean
You who are the dance of the sea
I call to you
ancient one
blessed goddess
Hear my voice
and come.
[Wait till She comes]
I give thanks
She is here.

Moon in Gemini

(Element: Air)

This is the best time to work communication magic, either through writing, teaching or selling. It is also a great time to do rituals that will increase your knowledge about anything that you need to assist you with your life. Ruled by Mercury, if you want more humour in your life, asking for it during a moon in Gemini will guarantee your successful attainment. For healing, focus on the nervous system, lungs, shoulders, arms and hands.

Benten is all mind and creativity. She will inspire your ritual during the moon in Gemini.

Oh Divine Sea Goddess
Benten
Immortal beautiful one
Protector of children
Bringer of wealth and prosperity

Bestower of inspiration
Goddess who gives with eight open hands
I sing your praises
with words of jade and pearls
Come and be with me
wise
wondrous
Benten
[Wait till She comes]
I give thanks
She is here.

Moon in Cancer

(Element: Water)

Be sure to use this time for lots of mermaid magic activities because the moon in Cancer is the ideal time for them. This is also a wonderful time to spend on rituals concerning your feelings, as the sign of Cancer rules the emotions and anything relating to the home, such as finding the best one! For healing, focus on mothering wounds, the breasts, stomach and solar plexus.

Yemanja is the mermaid goddess to make your magic deep and nurturing when the moon is in Cancer.

Mother O Goddess
O Yemanja
Mother Ocean
Mother of All
Take me in your arms
Rock me
Take me in your arms
Carry me
Take me in your arms
Comfort me
Mother I surrender
O Come.
[Wait till She comes]
I give thanks
She is here.

Moon in Leo

(Element: Fire)

This is the time to work leadership magic, especially if you want your company, project or committee to get out into the world with pizazz! If you are desiring to bring more creativity into your life, Sun-ruled Leo will ignite your ritual and turbo-charge your success. For healing, focus on the heart and the spine.

Strong-willed and intense **Ratu Rara Kidul** can be called upon to work with you when the moon is in Leo. This mermaid goddess has a special affinity for power and leadership, creativity and love.

> *Beloved Queen of the South Seas*
> *Mother Goddess Supreme*
> *With head bowed with respect*
> *and with all appropriate words of praise*
> *of your beauty and generosity*
> *kindness and benevolence*

your supplicant
on bended knee
invites your royal presence
and humbly entreats
that you come and be with me.
[Pause – wait for Her to arrive]
I give thanks
She is here.

Moon in Virgo

(Element: Earth)

If work is the issue that is needing your attention, be it right livelihood or a better job in the work that you love, then you will want to make magic when the moon is in Mercury-ruled Virgo. Anything connected to serving others and health would greatly benefit from some magical attention during this time. For healing, focus on the digestive system in its entirety.

Hina's vast knowledge of healing and ability to serve her people with her marvellous life-sustaining gifts can be of great help for rituals done during the moon in Virgo.

Glorious
breathtaking Hina
Hina of the honey-coated skin
Hina of the bounteous names
and guises
Hina generous gifter of seaweed
fish
and coconut
Waft your warm presence
like a tropical breeze
over me
Healer supreme
of knowledge from the watery deeps
Come and join me
[Wait for Her to arrive]
I give thanks
She is here.

Moon in Libra

(Element: Air)

This is the time *par excellence* to do relationship magic: for bringing romance into your life, for creating win-win situations in all your relationships, for healing any relationship challenges or glitches. Partnership and marriage will also profit from concentration during the moon in Venus-ruled Libra. If you find your need for justice aroused, whether you are involved in an upcoming court case or are finding injustice intolerable, this is the time for rituals to call it in. For healing, focus on the kidneys.

Atargatis will bring her fertilizing power to all rituals performed when the moon is in Libra.

> *Oh Great Fish Mother*
> *Atargatis*
> *You who are crowned*
> *with eagles*
> *and fly with the doves*

You who are the
companion of dolphins
and mother to countless fish in the sea
You who know the depths,
the dark side and destructive power
and the heights
the light and searing ecstacy
of love
Oh wise Atargatis
Come and be with me.
[Wait till She comes]
I give thanks
She is here.

Moon in Scorpio

(Element: Water)

When the moon is in Mars and Pluto-ruled Scorpio, the time favours rituals for transformation, regeneration and sexual expression. Since passion and desire are strong keynotes of the sign of Scorpio, if you find yourself a bit of a light-weight in these areas, then you may want to choose this time for magic making. For healing, focus on the reproductive system and rectum.

The passion and intensity of **La Sirene** is a perfect match for your magic during the moon in Scorpio.

La Belle Sirene
I offer you honeyed words
of praise
Your spell binding beauty
Your sinuous grace
The largeness of your heart
Your love
delicious beyond compare
I am your slave
I promise you a party
I promise you a feast
I promise you my love
if you will come to me
[Wait until She appears]

I give thanks
She is here.

Moon in Sagittarius

(Element: Fire)

This time is perfect for doing magic around travel: any-where you want to go, with or without your body! If you are wanting to get higher education or complete any edu-cation, the moon in Jupiter-ruled Sagittarius is the time for you to do your rituals. For healing, focus on the hips and thighs.

Benten of the eight-open-hands, known to seekers of higher knowledge, will charge any magic performed when the moon is in Sagittarius.

Oh Divine Sea Goddess
Benten
Immortal beautiful one
Protector of children

Bringer of wealth and prosperity
Bestower of inspiration
Goddess who gives with eight open hands
I sing your praises
with words of jade and pearls
Come and be with me
wise
wondrous
Benten
[Wait till She comes]
I give thanks
She is here.

Moon in Capricorn

(Element: Earth)

When the moon is in Saturn-ruled Capricorn, you will want to do rituals for organization (as in getting your life, closet or company better organized), anything to do with big business interests and creating economic security. This is also the time to invoke the Capricornian slogan of 'nothing can stop me now' to ensure that anything you undertake has the staying power to succeed. For healing, focus on the skeletal system, the skin and the knees.

Mere-Ama, compassionate water mother, bringer of fruitfulness of all She touches, consents to make strong magic with you when the moon is in Capricorn.

Dearest Mere-Ama
Water mother Divine
She who makes the crops
fertile
the fish and animals
fertile
and human beings
fertile
She of the wise hair
and knowing aspect
She who lovingly takes care
of those who seek her
Come and join me

Come and eat this food I have
prepared in your honour
Come and have your favourite drink.
[Wait until She appears]
I give thanks
She is here.

Moon in Aquarius

(Element: Air)

For getting your original ideas out into the world and for humanitarian pursuits and group work there is no better time for your magic than when the moon is in Uranus-ruled Aquarius. If you are seeking your independence from a relationship, job or your family, or leading a rebellion against the status quo, committing to heaps of rituals at this time will aide you in getting what you want. For healing, focus on your ankles and the circulatory system.

Jurate, lover of humanity, agrees to assist your workings of lunar magic when the moon is in Aquarius.

Radiant Jurate
She who watches over her people
and provides abundant fish
Lover of humanity
Goddess of the Sea
Beautiful
independent
One
Come and join me
now.
[Wait for Her to arrive]
I give thanks
She is here.

Moon in Pisces

(Element: Water)

This is the most auspicious time to work at changing your beliefs. (A good time for gaining clarity on what they are is when the moon is in Gemini.) If you are seeking to create retreat and renewal in your life, or to call in more compassion, do your magic when the moon is in Neptune and Jupiter co-ruled Pisces. For healing, focus on the feet.

Liban would be willing to come to your aide for mermaid magic when the moon is in Pisces. Her invocation follows:

> *Lovely*
> *loyal*
> *Liban*
> *Beloved*
> *of those with*
> *fur, fins and tails*
> *Deep and wise maiden*
> *of the salmon skin*
> *Come with your healing ways*
> *Come with your enchanting eyes*
> *Come Liban*
> *soulful One*
> *with compassion for all*
> *Come*

and bless me with your presence.
[Wait until She appears]
I give thanks
She is here.

Notes

1 Barbara G. Walker. *The Woman's Encyclopedia of Myths and Secrets*, Harper and Row Publishers, 1983, p. 584

2 Lemuria was thought to be a continent with a unique civilization which was located in the Indian Ocean 150 million years ago and preceded Atlantis.

3 Barbara G. Walker. *The Woman's Encyclopedia of Myths and Secrets*, Harper and Row Publishers, 1983, p. 288.

4 *Ibid*. p. 585.

5 *Ibid*. p. 911.

6 Note: 'An archetype is a pre-existent form that is part of the inherited structure of the psyche common to

all people.' 'A Psychological View of Conscience', *Civilization in Transition, The Collected Works of C.G. Jung* 10, par. 847.

7 Meri Lao. *Sirens*, Park Street Press, Rochester, Vermont, 1998, p. 94.

8 'The Mermaid's Vengeance', *Popular Romances of the West of England: The Drolls, Traditions and Superstitions of Old Cornwall*, collected and edited by Robert Hunt, 1903.

9 *Ibid.*

10 *Ibid.*

11 *Ibid.*

12 *Ibid.*

13 This is the civilization who created the Greek Myths as we know them today.

14 The Goddess who represented the Feminine in all her aspects: the huntress who protected the animals, the virgin (whole and complete unto herself) who made love in the woods, and the midwife.

15 Wells, H.G. *The Sea Lady*, McFarland & Company, Inc., p. 95.

Resource Guide

FOR PURCHASING READY-MADE TAILS

http://www.merfolktails.com

http://www.mermaidrentals.com/swimtail.htm

FOR SELF-HARDENING CLAY

http://www.artsuppliesonline.com/catalog.cfm?cata_id=
6457

http://www.pshcanada.com/clay4.htm

FOR KELP, BLADDERWRACK & DULSE

I highly recommend the Maine Seaweed Company. They will ship anywhere and everywhere. The minimum order can get you all you need for the recipes in this book.

Contact them at:

http://www.alcasoft.com/seaweed/index.html

FOR IRISH MOSS

The Dolphin Sea Vegetable Company hand harvests seaweed from all over Ireland, including Irish moss, dulse and kombu. Contact them at:

http://www.irishseaweeds.com

You can also purchase Irish moss (plus bladderwrack and dulse) from the following website:

http://www.blessedherbs.com

FOR HENNA, MERMAID TATTOO STENCILS AND TEMPORARY TATTOOS

http://www.naturalexpressions.org
http://miva.comsvr.com/cgi-bin/mivavm?/
   merchant.mvc+Screen=SFNT&Store_Code=TLS

http://www.bytheplanet.com/Products/Henna/Henna.htm
http://henna-boy.co.uk

FOR MERMAID POWER NECKLACE

For polymer clay:

http://www.polymerclayexpress.com
http://www.polymerclay.com.au/index.html
http://www.polymerclaypit.co.uk

Another way to make faux amber:

http://www.polymerclayexpress.com/nove2002.html

All other ingredients can either be found locally or on-line.

Bibliography

BOOKS

Ann, Martha & Dorothy Myers Imel. *Goddesses in World Mythology: A Biographical Dictionary*, Oxford, Oxford University Press, 1995

Baker, Margaret. *Folklore of the Sea*, London, David & Charles, 1979

Climo, Shirley and Lisa Falkenstern. *A Serenade of Mermaids: Mermaid Tales from Around the World*, New York, Harper Trophy, 1999

Eisler, Riane. *The Chalice & the Blade*, San Francisco, Harper & Row, 1987

Graves, Robert. *The Greek Myths*, England, Penguin, 1960

Heaser, Sue. *The Polymer Clay Techniques Book*, Ohio, North Light Books, 2002

Johnson, Buffie. *Lady of the Beasts: The Goddess and Her Sacred Animals*, Vermont, Inner Traditions, 1994

Kelly, Jill, Ph.D. *Guardians of the Celtic Way*, Vermont, Bear & Co., 2003

Lao, Meri. *Sirens: Symbols of Seduction*, Vermont, Park Street Press, 1997

Leach, Marjorie. *Guide to the Gods*, California, ABC-CLIO, Inc., 1992

Marashinsky, Amy Sophia and Hrana Janto. *The Goddess Oracle: A Way to Wholeness through Goddess and Ritual*, London, Element, 2002

Monaghan, Patricia. *The New Book of Goddesses & Heroines*, Minnesota, Llewellyn Publications, 2000

Neylon, Margaret. *Angel Magic*, London, Element, 2002

Osborne, Mary Pope, illustrated by Troy Howell. *Mermaid Tales from Around the World*, New York, Scholastic Inc., 1993

Piggott, Juliet. *Japanese Mythology*, London, Hamlyn, 1983

Rosser, Kip. *A Practical Book of Everyday Miracles*, Pennsylvania, Shade Publishing, 2004

Walker, Barbara G. *The Woman's Encyclopedia of Myths and Secrets*, San Francisco, Harper & Row, 1983

Wells, H. G., Edited by Leon Stover. *The Sea Lady: A Tissue of Moonshine: A Critical Text of the 1902 London First Edition, with an Introduction and Appendices*, North Carolina, McFarland & Company, 2001

Yeats, W. B. *Irish Fairy & Folk Tales*, New York, Barnes & Noble, 1993

Yolen, Jane and Shulamith Oppenheim. *The Fish Prince and Other Stories: Mermen Folk Tales*, Northampton, Interlink Publishing Company, 2001

VIDEO

Recreating Amber & Coral with Fimo, Volume 11, with Tory Hughes, California, Gameplan/ArtRanch, 1994

WEBSITES

http://www.belladonna.org/mermaidsexist.html
http://www.connexions.co.uk/culture/html/mz.htm
http://www.en.wikipedia.org/wiki/Melusine
http://www.endicott-studio.com/jMA03Summer/
    theMermaid.html
http://www.geocities.com/Athens/6415/yemanja.html
http://www.harvestmoon.net/Vodou/Lwa/LaSirene/
    lasirene.html
http://www.healthy.net/scr/article.asp?ID=1403
http://www.humanity.org/voices/folklore/mermaids/
http://www.isidore-of-seville.com/mermaids/3.html
http://www.jackowitch.com/mermaids1.html
http://www.lithuanian.net/resource/myths.htm
http://www.mermaid.net
http://www.mythicimages.com/printsea.htm
http://www.northstargallery.com/mermaids/
    MermaidHistory2.htm
http://www.occultopedia.com/m/mermaid.htm
http://www.onmarkproductions.com/html/
    benzaiten.shtml

http://www.orkneyjar.com/folklore/sea.html

http://www.peacecorps.gov/wws/guides/lithuania/
    lithgem.html

http://www.pitt.edu/~dash/melusina.html

http://www.powersthatbe.com/goddess/hawaiian/
    hina.html

http://www.sacred-texts.com

http://www.sochaczewski.com/
    ARTsultanandmermaid.html

http://www.whiterosesgarden.com/Enchanted_Waters/
    EW_content_pgs/EW_INDEX_PG.htm

http://www.widdershins.org/vol4iss8/01.htm

http://www.wordiq.com/definition/Mermaid

Amy Sophia Marashinsky is the author of *The Goddess Oracle: A Way to Wholeness through the Goddess and Ritual* with artist Hrana Janto. Prior to beginning her career as an author of books and oracles, Amy Sophia was an award-winning film-maker, a writer/director/producer of theatre in New York City, and had written and broadcast for NHK radio in Japan.

In addition to a love affair with mythology and fairy tales (which began when she was ten) and creating delicious food, Amy Sophia has counselled clients – one-to-one and relationships – facilitated past life regressions, done intuitive readings, and mediated and taught women's empowerment workshops for over 12 years. She currently devotes herself to a wide range of book and oracle projects at her home in Western Massachusetts. Visit her on the web: http://www.amysophia.com

A downloadable digital file of the journeys in *Mermaid Magic* is available from Amy Sophia Marashinsky. Email her at: info@mermaidmagic.net